Memories of family and estate:

Lithuania in the early 1900's

Memories of family and estate:
Lithuania in the early 1900's

Jonas Fledzinskas (1885-1965)

Translated from Lithuanian to English by Ruta Pempe Sevo

with Vytautas Fledzinskas & Sophie Pempe

Published in the USA. ISBN 978-0-9831588-2-0 paperback

Photographs are from family albums.
Cover design by Ruta Sevo.

Original in Lithuanian:
Fledzinskas, Jonas (1997). Atsiminimai: medziaga istorija.
Siauliai, Lietuva: Siauliu "Ausros" Muziejus. Redaktoriu
Kolegija: Eugenija Jovaisaite and Eugenija Raguckiene.
Dailininke: Vita Andruliene. Leidybos Vadove: Virginija
Siuksciene. ISBN 9986-766-06- 0. 119 pages (5" x 7.5"
paperback)

Publication of the memoir by Ausros Museum in Siauliai was
approved and financially sponsored by three children of J.
Fledzinskas living in America: Aleksandra Kasuba, Sofija
Pempe, and Vytautas Fledzinskas. The original text was
transcribed by Guoda Kasuba Burr. The publication was
prepared and supervised by Aleksandra Fledzinskaite Kasuba.

Original available from Siauliu "Ausros" Muziejus, Vytauto
89, 5419 Siauliai, Lithuania

English Translation:
Fledzinskas, Jonas (2010). Memories of family and estate:
Lithuania in the early 1900's. Translated from Lithuanian into
English by Ruta Pempe Sevo with Vytautas Fledzinskas &
Sophie Pempe.

About Ruta Pempe Sevo at momox.org

My grandfather died in 1965 in Skaudvile, Lithuania. At the time, I was 20 years old and in college, while my parents lived in Seattle, Washington, USA. I never met him. Lithuania was under Russian occupation with highly controlled borders until 1991, the year it finally reached political independence. I could not have afforded the travel until the 1980's, anyway. He was lost to me due to our life circumstances and timing.

My parents fled in 1945 with the German occupiers, who were being pushed out by the returning Russians. They were refugees in Germany on the last day of World War II in Europe, which was the day I was born (May 7/8, 1945). Once they left their homeland, they lived a life permanently separate from their parents and many relatives. My mother's sister and one brother emigrated and lived in the same cultural exile, all eventually in America.

When the Russians were pushed out of Lithuania by the Germans in 1941/42, they left behind lists of people to be deported to Siberia. The lists included the names of any nobles, civil servants, teachers, religious leaders, and basically anyone with higher education. The fate of those who stayed and suffered deportation to Siberia is well known – they were worked and starved to near-death for decades. It was a policy of slow extermination (as opposed to the German treatment of Jews). (Russia traditionally used deportation instead of imprisonment to dispose of undesirables.) If my parents had not left, I would probably be dead.

The émigrés were all glad to escape the fate they

might have met in Lithuania and found much opportunity in America. (It's true: life is good in America.) My family lived in Utah, Idaho, and Seattle apart from our ethnic community in America. My mother taught her two oldest children to read, and we spoke "kitchen" Lithuanian at home. My parents were very hard-working immigrants with five children to feed. There was little time to remember and tell their experiences in the homeland and in their youth. We heard little about what transpired and even little about the pleasures of happy times in their youth.

Recovering their past and Lithuanian language and culture was not a priority for me as I navigated an American education and jobs. Finally I visited, at the age of 52, in 1997, after Lithuania was opened to the world and receiving tourists freely. It was fascinating and overwhelming to absorb everything that had been locked away: family ties, family stories, history and current conditions of Lithuania. I felt like an adoptee discovering her origins and redefining her identity. There was a feeling of tremendous discovery along with uncovered pain for the love we could have had, a family life richer and deeper than growing up in exile and separation. The experience of intellectual rediscovery of Lithuania is recalled in my short novel *Vilnius Diary* (available online on amazon.com).

My grandfather's memoir appeared in print in 1997. My mother and her siblings had the memoir in possession and sponsored its publication by the Ausros Museum in Siauliai. Once I learned of it, I was excited to see it, but did not have the time it would take to struggle to read it in Lithuanian.

I became a Ph.D. Asian scholar along the way and

learned four additional languages, including German, Bengali and Sanskrit. I translated three Bengali novels (supported by a PEN Translation Fellowship in 1973) and did enjoy slogging through a foreign text with a fat dictionary. Once I recovered more conversational Lithuanian I thought I could tackle my grandfather's memoir. As a modern narrative, it had to be easier than Sanskrit poetry. Now there are automatic translators on the internet that can supplement the fat dictionary. I did most of the work over ten days in Vilnius (ten pages a day), camped in a small room in a former convent, during a cold November. My uncle and my mother stepped in to correct translation errors and forms of names. I will never be fluent, but it remains the language that throws me back to childhood.

(FYI the J. Fledzinskas family was at least quadra-lingual, coming from families speaking Polish and Russian, with study in Germany, and then adopting Lithuanian as their home language.)

The memoir was disappointing in its impersonality. Compared with modern confessional writing in America, there is very little about family secrets, passions, mistakes, and deep motivations. How do I explain that to myself? Europeans and especially Russians, I hear, tend to be more private than Americans and put on a positive public face by habit. Some people are not emotional by personality and their heads really are filled with facts, business ideas, and activities instead of feelings.

My grandfather does not dwell on emotional memories of family life, the daily delights of raising children, the influences of elders, relationships with workers, and such. Politically, my grandfather and grandmother were at risk of being deported to Siberia because of her heritage as a Countess and an estate owner. They were spared exile due to the intervention of loyal friends, but they lost ownership of the large family estate. He was clearly a socialist and believed in a cooperative, socialist economic system, so he may have been intellectually in agreement with the transfer of property to the Land Trust.

He was also "on the list of those to exile" with the Russians and could not reveal everything he thought about the occupation in his memoir, which was finished in 1959, still during the occupation. He probably had to live below the radar politically, even in the small town of Skaudvile. Anyone associated with nobles, or especially married to one, hid from public attention. He displays no sense of injustice or anger toward the authorities. He emphasizes positives and conveys his excitement about the early development of agricultural and growth of exports from Lithuania. It is not an introspective exploration of his life.

Still, not many people leave a piece of themselves in writing. I am grateful to have this piece of him, and apologize if there are still errors of translation. The little book is my memorial to him.

Ruta Pempe Sevo,
the daughter of his daughter Sofija
Fledzinskaite-Pempe, May 2010

THANKS:
To my uncle (and son of Jonas Fledzinskas), Vytautas Fledzinskas, for several long, careful readings

and many corrections to the translation. To my mother (and daughter of Jonas Fledzinskas), Sofija Fledzinskaite-Pempe in Seattle, WA, for sharing the memoir, for her help with facts and translations, and for photographs. Photos were scanned by Werner and Saulius Pempe.

Appreciation to Erika Melamed in Vilnius, Lithuania, who helped me navigate the homeland as a stranger.

To Eugenia Kienciene, a marvelous historian living in Skaudvile, who greeted two strangers one night and shared her knowledge as a friend of the Fledzinskas family. She tended the Fledzinskas' grave site and published a history of Skaudvile.

To Dainius Sukys in Siauliai, Lithuania, who compiled and shared extensive genealogical research of the Zubov family tree including the Fledzinskas branch.

TABLE OF CONTENTS

Chapter 1

Early memories. Home, family. Mother's activities. Childish pursuits. Relatives and neighbors.

I have trouble picturing my father. For years (1888-1889) he worked in Kybartai and visited us only from time to time. My mother lived in Skaudvile with four children, in the same house where I live now. I can picture my older brother Vytautas, their first child, who was about 20 years old, had a job, and was out on his own. My older sister Stase (who later married Stankevicius) was about 15 years old, Juzefa, about 11-12 years, Ona, 8-9 years, and I, the youngest, was 3-4 years old.

My first clear memory is a spinning toy. It is early in the morning. I am standing in the doorway of a big room (the path from the kitchen) and with great glee watch the jumping, noisy toy. My father sits in a chair next to the window, where the thermometer is located now. I don't remember his face. He had arrived late the night before and brought me the long-awaited gift made of bone. He wound it up and released it as I entered the room.

That was my last visit with my father. The next thing, he was in America, with no warning to my mother. It was only several years later that he started writing to my mother and sending her small amounts of money.

I remember my mother as worn out, tired, and often tearful. Her beautiful face (much like Aunt Juzefa's) comes to mind. It wasn't easy to stay committed to the marriage and not easy to feed four children. We had our own little house on a rather large 75 pieces of land. Mother kept cows and piglets, but that was not enough to feed us. Thankfully, she was a homeopathic healer with a huge following and a good reputation in the region around Skaudvile. Medicines came from Batakiai, Erzvilkas and other surrounding villages. I think her advice helped a lot of people because, along with the medicine, she insisted on a room isolated for the sick person, in which it was forbidden to smoke, and prescribed a light, no-fat diet for the patient.

Homeopathy provided the main sustenance for our family. A lot of sick people came by, especially Tuesdays (market day), and Sundays. Every patient paid 20 kopecs for medicine. I remember my mother bragging that she brought in more than 3 rubles on a given Tuesday. You have to know that 3 rubles was a huge amount at the end of the 19th century. At that time, 400 grams of butter cost 18-20 kopecs (at 45-50 kopecs a kilogram), 10 eggs were 15-16 kopecs, veal was 5-6 kopecs. Perfect pretzels (the likes of which people don't know how to make) cost 1 kopec. For 3 rubles you could buy a lot of food and other goods.

Aside from homeopathy, my mother earned money making quilts, with the help of her daughters, her sisters, and Aunt Tekle. She was very hard-working, frugal, resourceful, and took competent care of the family in every way.

2

Toward the end of the 1900, my older sister Stase took a job near Petersburg so that I could go to school. She regularly sent part of her salary to my mother to pay for my schooling in Raseiniai district. After a few years working, she returned to Skaudvile, married Stankevicius and moved away to Jekaterinoslavo with him, where he worked in the Jenakijevo metals factory. My second sister Juzefa was taught to sew. She started her own embroidery business to earn money and spent just about her whole life in Skaudvile.

My younger sister Ona finished Skaudvile's public school and started teaching. She was the first woman to attend the school. Her first assignment was at Silo Pavezupis in the Putvinskis estate (the father of Stasys), who ran an underground Lithuanian school since 1905. She started to prepare for a teacher's certification on her own. It was hard. With great determination, she took the external exams in Petersburg and got her certificate.

My older brother Vytautas suddenly got T.B. and died at the start of the 20th Century. A few years later my mother died too.

Thinking back on the more pleasant things that happened in my youth, I remember trips for lessons to Zakariske, Noriske, and Zuikiske. The people who ran Zakariske were the Daujotai, the parents of S. Slavinskiene, both very nice and easy going. My mother was good friends with Mrs. Daujotiene. She often traveled to Skaudvile for various farm matters and always visited with us. Sometimes she took my mother and me back to Zakariske with her. Mrs. Daujotas had a daughter named Stefa, who is now Stefa Slavinskiene, with whom I played and kidded around. I traveled to Zakariske on my own a lot too. I really had a good time there: I got to ride a horse, harvest hay and wheat, go fishing, pick berries, and do a lot of other farm things.

I was allowed to go to Zakariske alone even though I was only 7-8 years old. Part of the way was across fields and pastures. Sometimes I wanted to scare the animals. I had to climb over a fence to a pasture with cows and bulls. After I climbed over the fence and went a few steps, I saw that a huge bellowing bull was charging me. I turned and ran back to the fence and don't even remember how I got over it. The charging bull hit the fence so hard that it fell over. I jumped, tripped, fell down, and then ran away. The surprised bull stayed there.

The old, large-boned widow Mrs. Rakauskas lived on the Noriske farm. Her oldest daughter and her children would come to visit for summer vacation. Two boys were roughly my age. Right after they arrived at Noriske they would come to Skaudvile to get me. I would visit them about 10 times over a few weeks. It was so much fun! We did whatever we wanted! I have a lot of good memories of running around in the woods and the friendly farm people.

My father's family owned a small piece of land – no more than 20 acres – in Zuikiske, on the outskirts of Pagramantis. At that time, three sisters and brothers lived there. The farm was very well maintained: a new, comfortable house with clean and cozy rooms. There was a huge orchard next to the house, just beyond that a narrow gorge with a flowing creek called Pakrazantis. Next to the creek were hills covered with trees and bushes. One slightly bigger hill drew my interest in particular because it was said that there were caves in the hill holding valuable ancient treasures. There was a spell on the treasure keeping people away from it. The secrets of this hill really worked my imagination.

The people living around it were interesting. One was my father's older sister Aunt Mare, an old spinster, good humored, and very spiritual. The walls of her room bore religious pictures, there was an altar before which she prayed and worshipped a lot. She wore only black, constantly recited the rosary and fasted. Her much younger sister Magdalena was strong, heavy, and energetic and took care of the farm. Her beauty and her personality always fascinated me. They both spoke only Lithuanian and did not know any other language. My uncle Stasys, my father's brother, was a bachelor who lived with them. He was very lively and nice, full of fun and good humored. He spent a lot of time lying in bed because he had sores on his feet. They all loved us children, feeding us nuts and honey. We got very tasty apples from them. We weren't there much because it was hard to get there and we didn't have any means of transportation. I walked a few times but it was a long journey.

There was yet another brother of my father's – Juozas. I barely remember what he looked like and don't remember where he lived. His daughter Stefa married Gostautas and had seven sons. Birute, the daughter of their son Jonas, lives with us now. She is 9 years old and goes to school.

Studies in Skaudvile and Raseiniai. Employment. Children going to school at Uteliai estate, training in pharmacy. Bookkeeping and administrative jobs in Ringuvenai, Nerimdaiciai, and Nevarenai lumber mills.

I finished primary school in Skaudvile very quickly. I don't remember much from that time. Except when, one evening, a Russian teacher came to visit. At that time we lived in an extension of the school. I was in the kitchen. Suddenly my mother came into the kitchen and said, with tears in her eyes, that the teacher came to reprimand me. He said I was lazy, unruly, and my homework was messy. He offered to beat me with a switch. My mother's tears, or maybe the threat of a stick, impressed me so much that from that day on I started to study seriously, racing through the early grades and finished in five. I remember once, a visiting inspector asked in school "Who rules Finland?" and I answered wrong. (At the time it belonged to the Russians.) The teacher could not forgive me for a long time.

I dreamed of going to college even before starting school. I really wanted to learn. My mother thought about college too. Her brother Jonas Jokubauskas (the father of Aunt Niuta) served in Liepoja's customs and had promised my mother he would take me in and send me to college with his children. But when I entered the third grade, he died, suddenly, leaving a big family without a caretaker and without a source of income. My hope for college died too.

At that time my mother's brother Kostas came to visit. He was a large-scale farmer and very well off. I think he lived with his wife and one daughter on his wife's farm, in the area outside Raseiniai. While he was at our house one day, my mother called me to them. He said that he would send me to college, if I promised to study to be a priest. It was not easy for me to decline. At that time I was very devout – serving at mass, going to confession a lot, saying long prayers when I went to bed at night. I guess the idea of being a priest was not scary. It's just that I didn't want to. Maybe it was because it depended on support from my uncle Kostas, and I didn't like him – and even was afraid of him. I cried when I told my mother I did not want to be a priest.

Let me explain that since there was no hope of sending me to high school, it was decided that I would go to a public school in Raseiniai. My older sister Stase helped a lot with that after she found a job and promised my mother she would support my schooling. I graduated when I was 13 years old. I started to work immediately so I would not be a burden to my mother, but I kept dreaming about going to high school. I bought high school texts and studied them, thinking that I could pass the first through fourth exams, and then all eight.

My first job was at the farm in Uteliai (not far from Kryzkeliai). I taught two of the owner's children, preparing them for high school. I was there through the fall into winter. Early in the spring, I returned to Skaudvile because my students no longer had time to study. They had to help with farm work, and besides, their parents thought they had learned enough.

While I lived in Uteliai I first started to doubt my faith. I don't remember what prompted that. It wasn't that I had a huge crisis of conscience from reading books. The people I was living with could not explain things to me. I sought out the priest and was rudely rebuked and sent off without any insight. In effect that pushed me away from the church. The priest advised me to say certain prayers for two weeks and come back to confession. I never went to confession again. I felt released from the calling.

While I was back in Skaudvile living with my mother, I helped the pharmacist Raciunas. I could not help a lot because I wasn't trained in it and did not like the work.

A woman we knew offered me a job at the Ringuvenai farm (4 kilometers from Kursenai, near the Papile road) with the tenants Parazinski. They wanted me to be a tutor and be a companion to their 5 or 6 year old son. I was in Ringuvenai the whole summer into late fall. Then his mother took over care of the boy again, and the farm manager offered me work in the lumber mill office.

I went to Nerimdaiciai (9 kilometers from Tryskiai town) to the forest where the sawmill was located. I didn't have a lot of work to do and thus could spend a lot of time with my books. There were a lot of hunters in Nerimdaiciai who kept hounds and knew the hunting territory. The forest owner Gorskis would come in the fall and winter to hunt. He brought his friends and a pack of hounds. We hunted from early morning to late evening.

We would come back at night with a few rabbits and sometimes a fox or wild deer.

A parish priest in Nerimdaiciai helped me finish a high school course in Latin. In the middle of my study we took up playing cards which I did not know, but I was able to learn quickly. This led me (alas!) to something much more interesting than Latin. We started a regular card game and spent a lot of time around a little green table.

When the lumber mill job in Nerimdaiciai ended, I went to work in Nevarenai again in a sawmill, but this time as a manager. There wasn't time to hunt, play cards, or study. I had to work from dusk to dawn. I had to take care of the logistics of bringing in lumber, loading it for transport to the railway station, overseeing the mill, and doing the accounts. I often slept just 4-5 hours. I ate supper only on Sundays, which I prepared myself, because the woman in charge of the kitchen was messy and really dirty. When I left for work early in the morning, I ate a piece of raw ham and drank boiled milk. At night I cooked potatoes with bacon fat and sometimes some barley. On Sundays I made a soup of meat broth with rice and had savory pancakes with berries. The job in Nerimdaiciai did not last long. I settled with the owner and returned to Skaudvile.

Chapter 3

To Jenakijev. Belgian corporation. Administration, management, and workers. Underground work. General strike of factory workers. Fired from job.

My older sister Stase married Stankevicius and lived in Jenakijev (in Jekaterin province, around Bachmuto). Her husband was manager of a factory warehouse. They invited me to come to Jenakijev and promised to see about a job in the factory. In the spring of 1903 I went to them.

Jenakijev was a large metals factory. It had a copper mine and two coal mines. There were 5,000 workers in the factory alone. The director, some managers and supervisors were Belgians, and Poles staffed the office with a few Lithuanians. The workers were local Russians. The factory was built with Belgian capital, so most of the stock belonged to the Belgians. Records were maintained in French. The CEO was a Belgian.

The factory was located in the countryside. To house both administrators and workers, they built varous buildings. One of them – three stories high – was called "the insane asylum." It was for single upper-level people. The first floor had a library, restaurant and various rooms for men and guards. The second and third floors were designed for the single life: a system of corridors, mostly small rooms, and lavatories. Everyone who lived there could get furniture from the factory inventory for a token payment. There were about 30 single men living there, mostly young men who worked in various factory offices. Shortly after I arrived in Jenakijev I got a job in bookkeeping and a room in "the insane asylum."

I quickly got to know a few residents. There were serious and friendly. We went for walks, talking and arguing mostly about politics. I found that my new acquaintances were left-leaning fellows who seemed very compatible and like-minded. Before long we agreed to form a social-democratic group.

The first thing I wanted to do was get conversant with the issues that were most frequently raised with the managers. I wanted to understand the fundamentals of a capitalist system. Older friends suggested I study sociology, cultural history, political economy, and the works of Marx. We had an older Marxist in our group who was an intellectual and free thinker. He led our party meetings and helped us clarify questions that were vague or confusing. He gave us material to read. It did not take long for me to become the de facto leader. The Russian revolution was starting during that time. We had to raise the worker's awareness quickly and organize them. To that end there were small, closed worker groups and each was assigned a mentor. He read and explained the newspapers and party position papers to the workers. Sometimes we got to read the social-democratic newspaper "Iskra" issued in Switzerland with the workers.

I had a few workers assigned to me too. We met once or twice a week at one of their homes, or in the summer in the field or in the hills. I really liked it. The workers paid good attention to explanations of the issues. If the group was not betrayed, the activity was not very dangerous. Once in a while a police agent or spy infiltrated, and inevitably the groups' activities were severely constrained.

Besides working with workers it fell to me to prepare and distribute leaflets. The content of the leaflets was usually lifted from "Iskra," about things related to factories and workers. The leaflets had to be printed by hand and duplicated using a hectograph. I could get about 50-60 copies. It took 3-4 hours to do a leaflet. Those were dangerous hours. We often got help to put them out and distribute them. We scattered them then at the front entry gate or by the workers' housing, some we put on fences, and sometimes we dared to hand them out personally. I was risking it both preparing and distributing, but nothing bad happened.

The building for singles got known as a den of revolutionaries. When the police looked for a resident, they would search everybody there. On one raid they found a hectograph in the eaves but could not tell who used it.

A few times we had some tense minutes. A saw operator in the factory next door to me made little boxes for grenades and kept them under his bed. One day, he showed them to me and said, both cautiously and complaining, that his organization (social revolutionaries) would not accept the boxes. The next evening, I was in the hall and saw three police standing in front of his door knocking. A little later I saw my neighbor – meaning, he had been home. "I thought they had me there, for a minute." But the police standing at his door saw me and asked where my neighbor was. I said he wasn't home. They waited an hour and then left. That evening I told my neighbor who came to see him and wanted to know where he was. It turns out he saw them coming and he figured out they might be after him, so he locked his door from the inside and climbed out the window, and jumped from the second story. That's how he saved himself – the police were not allowed to search if the owner was not there.

In 1905 there was a general strike among factory workers everywhere. The strike was purely political; economic issues were not leveraged. The factory management organized a meeting and after a lot of debate, they came to a consensus to strike with the workers. Not one came to work. The strike was truly general and appeared to be well organized. The factory owners were very worried about the goals of the strike because there was increasing danger that it could cover a much bigger flame.

Several strike-breakers had already been beaten up by the workers. The administration tried to diffuse the strike starting with the supervisors. They were all called to the administrators' meeting room (since there were about 100 supervisors) and lined up. The senior Belgian director who represented several layers of management, went to each supervisor and asked each one if he was on strike, or not on strike. Unfortunately, whereas we had decided to strike together, now, so as not to scare the director, each declared that they were not striking and only a few – five or six of us – declared we were on strike. After he spoke with all the supervisors, the Director instructed that the strikers were all to be relieved of their duties and all those not striking should go back to work. They went back to work and we, those fired, were now without a job. In one more day the workers' strike ended too. The workers managed to get their laid-off friends back on the job. Nobody fended for the supervisors who were laid off. I had no job, because there were no jobs outside the factory.

Chapter 4

Armed revolt in Goriovko region. Clash with Cassocks.
Victims and their funerals.

Once, an armed fight broke out between the
workers and the police, and armed cells of workers were
formed in the factory and in the mines. Those who dared
attacked the police and even army soldiers. For example,
at a mine nearby, the workers overtook a whole company
of soldiers and took their weapons and their overcoats.
The leader of those workers was a school teacher – a social
revolutionary. A short time after that he and his wife were
killed in an encounter in Gorlovko. The group in our
factory did not particularly seek militancy and did not
have weapons or a leader. Generally, the militant and
armed social democrats were considerably weaker than
the social revolutionaries.

About that time we heard that the militant
rebellion had an important mission to accomplish and
they were to meet secretly at the Gorlovko station. A train
was sent to the rail station at our factory, and it was
supposed to carry the armed group to Gorlovko. At the
designated time, about ten of us gathered at the train
station. Only a few had army rifles. Others were
promised weapons in Gorlovko. When the train arrived,
we boarded into several wagons. In Gorlovko there was
supposed to be an unarmed army company, and from
there the operation was to move toward Jekaterinoslav. A
lot of workers had gathered at Gorlovko but they were like

15

us – unarmed and unprepared for an attack. Only a few dozen men were dressed in army coats and carried army rifles.

The station was under the control of the rebels. We entered the station at night. Every space in the station was so crowded that we had to stand all night. Weapons were not handed out.

Early in the morning several groups mobilized and we started the attack on the army. We found the surrounding barracks empty. The soldiers had been driven out and the barracks belonged to the rebels.

Around noon we heard shots from two sides up. We figured out that the station was being attacked by a formation of about 100 Cossacks.

They had arrived from Jenakijev where they had been guarding our factory. Bullets started to whistle from the station platform. The workers near the station, armed with military rifles, didn't see their leader, the social revolutionary, lying on the tracks near the entry to the second class waiting room, shooting it out with Cossacks who were attacking. At first I stood on the empty platform hugging the walls, and then I went inside. The shots were fast and furious as Cossacks appeared on the tracks as they shot toward the station building, where people were seeking cover from the bullets. When things quieted down, the Cossacks had the station. There were a few wounded workers, and some dead. Among the dead were the teacher and his wife, lying on the tracks.

They were both young and attractive, and had just met a few months before. I heard that the woman ran over to him when she couldn't hear any more shooting from him, and fell at his side almost immediately, shot by

Cossack bullets. They were both found dead. The teacher was a well-known social revolutionary.

When the shooting completely stopped, we were called to the platform and divided into two lines. There were fewer leaders among us than there had been before. We could not see the Cossacks. The army company, standing in one line, stood within 15-20 paces of us. They told us they would pick out every 5th or 10th man and hand him over to the Cossacks to be shot.

Suddenly the leader of the army stepped forward and spoke, standing between the workers and the soldiers. He was very dismayed that we were killing each other, committing a crime, when we are brothers who should live side by side, and we should part as friends, not enemies. He went up to one of the workers standing in line, offered his hand, hugged him, and kissed him. An unbelievable outcome! After that, they provided us a train to take us back to Jenakijev.

The next day we had a funeral for two of our factory workers from Gorlovko who had died. A lot of people came. The mood was positive. The funeral turned into a big ceremony. We bragged about our revolutionary days. A few revolutionary speeches were made over the graves of the dead. A large contingent from the hundred Cossacks and police attended and did not interfere with us, nor with the speeches over the graves.

Chapter 5

A trip to Bachmuto prison. The prison in Lugansko.
Life as a prisoner. Conflict with administrators. A
hunger strike. Interrogation. Exile from South Russia.

Arrests started a few days after the funeral. Men
were taken to the police station, questioned, and some
released immediately. Others were held. All those held
were transferred over to Cossack soldiers and transported
to the area surrounding Bachmuto. I ended up among
them. There were about 40 people, mostly factory
supervisors and workers and a few natives of Jenakiyev.
The Cossacks transporting us to Bachmuto were the same
ones whom we fought in Gorlovko.

There were wounded among them. The Cossacks
took every chance to take revenge on us, swearing and
beating. A very cold winter wind blew. They put 5-6 of
us in plain farmer's carts pulled by one horse. Three
Cossack guards rode in front. Angry and vengeful, they
looked for chances to hit the prisoners with the butts of
their rifles. We arrived at Bachmuto that night. Pretty
much every one of us was beaten up, cold, tired, and
extremely hungry, having not eaten since morning. Some
were so stiff from the cold that they could not climb out of
the cart by themselves. They were carried into the police
station and laid on the floor. These unfortunate men later
had problems with frozen hands and feet.

It turned out that Bachmuto prison was full and
there was no room for us. We had to move on to

Lugansko. We were put back into the wagons and transported that night. From the Lugansko station they took us to the prison which was far past the town. Exhausted, cold men could not walk, and some had to be carried. At the prison they roughly shook us down, taking away money, knives, mirrors, and even metal combs. They shoved us into two small rooms, about 20 in each. The rooms were big enough for just a few people – unheated, windows broken out, the floor a deep layer of frozen mud. Just a few people fit on a bench and the rest had to sit on the ground. Outside the windows we could see tall gallows meant to scare us. Tired, scared men started to moan and even cry. An old gentlemen from Jenakijev town – intelligent, cultured people, got hysterical. That made some mad and others worried. We were exhausted and in low spirits from the trip. The weaker men were put on the bench and us stronger ones lay down on the floor.

The next morning we did not have to be wakened. It was still dark and we were already awake, even more tired than the night before. My back hurt from the awful position, sides hurt, feet cold, chills up my back, face hurt from bites of some animal. The air was foul. We had stuffed rags into the windows.

We asked the guard whether we could prepare a set of "demands" he would deliver. He said it was too early and in time the door would be unlocked. A breakfast of hot water and bread was brought. We were so hungry that we ate the whole day's ration of bread. We drank the hot water without a bit of sugar or tea, and felt a little better. We started to clean up the mud from the floor – they would not give us water – and washed the walls. At lunch they brought soup and hot cereal. We were still starving and heartily ate the soup and cereal. In the evening we got mattresses, blankets and pillows. We found out that we could buy local produce with our money left in the office.

Local criminals came around to help us. Careful not to be seen by the guards, they came to our door and told us what was happening outside, and offered to advise us. We tried to get a larger room, through them. Some of our friends were in a nearby cell and we started corresponding. The inmates sincerely advised us and, to be honest, they really helped. There were very friendly men among them.

As soon as the second day of our incarceration there were conflicts with the guards. The most frequent reason for disagreements was that they would not open the door, as they were supposed to, to let the people out who had diarrhea. They did not let them go to the toilet. One guard, Cerber (the "Dog Devil"), stubbornly refused to open the door. We made a lot of noise, pounding a stool against the door and demanding to see the officer in charge. Other cells joined us. The whole corridor erupted in noise.

A representative of the chief officer arrived. The brawl stopped when we got a doctor, medicine, white bread for the sick, and even a bit of milk. We succeeded in getting more wooden stools and a bigger waste bucket. Even the rations of bread increased. It was good bread with flavor. We ran short of it all the time.

We got to know each other very well living so close in one room. There were some fine men among us. They started to tell endless stories about various underground operations. One gentleman from Jenakijev turned out to be a man who had been around and seen a lot. He was missing three fingers on his left hand. We asked him how he lost the fingers. He was quiet a long time, but eventually told us. He was trying to tame a lion, inside the cage with the lion. The lion attacked. He didn't pull his hand back in time as the lion's claws tore off his fingers.

There were a few literate workers among us too, it turned out, with whom we'd worked. We got newspapers to read. It was hard to write because we didn't have paper. Chess figures and checkers were made out of bread. We got along well as we waited to be interrogated and sentenced. We were well prepared for interrogations by Russian political prisoners of whom there seemed to be a lot.

One morning, maybe after a few weeks in jail, an older "Cerber" came to our room and called for me. He told me to gather my things and go with him. I asked if I was coming back and he said I was not. I put all my remaining food in my pockets and said good-bye to my friends. I was taken to the third story and put in a cell. Inside, I saw a young, good-looking, blond-haired man sitting on a stool, watching me with great interest. After the door shut I extended my hand and asked him who he was, and why in jail? He was really happy to have company. I found out that he was a well-known teacher, already several months in jail, accused of serious violations (I don't remember what kind), already interrogated, and waiting to be sentenced. There was no hope to prove his innocence.

The cell was lighter and cleaner than our common room. My new acquaintance seemed cultured and friendly. Things were looking better. After I got to know him better I decided he had a perfect baritone voice and that he probably sang popular or romantic songs. You were not allowed to sing in prison, but the guards allowed my companion, and asked him to just sing quietly, and they stood near our door and listened. His songs had a strong effect on us – some moved us to tears.

He wasn't able to stay long. After a few weeks, they led him away and I had no idea what happened. He was not in our prison any more. I was sorry for him and felt lonely, sensing what it is to be in prison. Anyway, I was tormented with worry about the fate of my new friend for a long time.

It is a big thrill to have family visit you in prison. My sister Ona, who moved in with my older sister in Jenakijev, visited me. Strangers came to visit me a few times to ask if I needed anything or to tell me what was going on outside. It wasn't possible to talk freely with visitors. Right there stood "Cerber" listening closely and saw that prisoners were not given anything. Nevertheless, after every visit I inevitably brought a letter, interesting newspaper clipping or even a whole newspaper back to my room. Even small amounts of money that make life in prison a little easier.

It was also a thrill to get little packages of food without spending money. I was not short of those – my sister provided all kinds of things. On Easter the people in Lugansko generously gave us eggs, meat, and cake ("kuliciai"). In one cake I found a bottle of vodka. I would find notes sending me greetings and good wishes. It was a great comfort to feel that people supported and sympathized with political prisoners. Girls who didn't know us came to the prison to wave scarves and flowers from a distance. We stood on tables so we could see them. It was summer outside – sweet & warm sunshine, greening grasses, brightly singing birds. It was painfully sad.

I was alone in the cell for a long time. They gave me a companion just before the end of June or July – an old Pole who only talked about his wife's cooking. It seems he was so starved for good food he could talk of nothing else. Being alone was the worst punishment. It was hard to be alone without work or books. Chopping wood, pumping water and other tasks in the prison yard seemed like a break. We wanted them and asked for them. Groups of 6 or 8 prisoners were put together for those jobs. We worked conscientiously, and managed to divide the work between the old hands and new. If we had a good "Cerber," we could decide how to handle things, and make up instructions. While we were in the prison yard, we decided to organize a hunger strike. I don't remember what issue prompted the idea of a strike. We started striking the next morning and stopped by lunch on the third day. The evening of the second day I had a really bad stomach ache. By the third I was weak and didn't want to get out of bed. The short hunger strike really made an impression on the prison chiefs and on the residents of Lugansko. There were a lot of people at the prison gates all the time, wanting to know what was going on. A prosecutor and doctors appeared at the prison. They promised that if we gave up the strike, they would look into our cases. We told them we would stop striking when the prison chiefs dropped the cases against us. After the strike we had a lighter routine and better food.

The interrogations started while I was still alone in the cell. All the prisoners from Jenakijev (and maybe others too) were instructed how to behave during interrogation and how to answer certain questions.

I realized from the very first interrogation that the interrogator knew nothing about my underground work at the factory, and that the only charge against me was for taking part in the armed revolt. This considerably prolonged my situation, because several hundred citizens were involved in the rebellion and the Gorlovko conflict was an insignificant episode in the beginning of the revolution. The prisons were full and that was why the officials could not complete the bureaucratic process. An interrogator at Gorlovko was sent from Petrograd (now Leningrad) for especially complex situations, to close the cases of insurgents.

He ended up complicating things. The prisoners denied participating in the uprising or explained that they had no weapons and therefore there was no law that applied for the armed rebellion. There were too few witnesses in these cases. Prospective witnesses had been severely reprimanded, or even killed.

At the end of the summer, we Jenakijev factory prisoners were released into police custody. When I arrived at Stankevicius, the police ordered me to leave South Russia immediately, go back to my home, and report to the police there. I figured that in Skaudvile, I would just have to check in with the local policeman, and it would not be hard to deal with him.

Chapter 6

I did not have a regular job when I got back to Skaudvile. I lived with my sister. Sundays and Tuesdays I walked to the clinic to help in the pharmacy. After a few weeks I happened to run into an old friend (from times in Jenakijev), K. Gruzdys, at his brother's farm not far from Kelme. It was a beautiful old farm of nice and honorable people in the old style. I was under police supervision but it was no bother. I had a deal with the supervisor that I would not check in with him as a routine, but if I had to leave Skauvile I would let him know. Thus my relationship with the police ended.

In the fall, somebody told me (I don't remember who or how) that there was an open bookkeeping position at Count Zubov's Ginkunai estate and that they offered it to me. I was instructed to go to Siauliai to the lawyer S. Lukauskis and I would meet Mr. Zubov there. At that time I had a poor grasp of bookkeeping and it was risky to take a position as a bookkeeper, but I was invited and had to go.

At the lawyer S. Lukauskis' office, I found two very nice and hospitable people. Especially Mrs. E. Luskauskiene. She served me a meal, along with very delicious cake, and told me a lot about the Zubovs in Ginkunai and managed to let me know there were two young ladies – the landowner's daughter and her school friend, with whom she goes to school. "Both girls are very pretty and very nice. Be careful you don't fall in love with one of them," she added.

She told me to take the job without reservation, and not to worry about knowing bookkeeping. In a little bit Mr. V. Zubov arrived. He was already familiar with me (and I still don't know who provided the information). He knew I'd been released from prison just recently. I guess the recommendations were enough for him. We talked only briefly. He did not seem to care that I didn't really know bookkeeping. He asked me to come to Ginkunai right after the Christmas holidays and take the job.

I left Siauliai with the highest hope and a good mood, but I did not sense that I had found a fine future.

I arrived in Ginkunai the first Sunday after the holidays. The coach was late coming into Siauliai. I found horses from Ginkunai at the post office (the region of Guberija) I got to Ginkunai about 8 o'clock. It was hard and intimidating to go into a strange place to live with complete strangers. I was greeted by a butler who received me in the hall, took my coat, and led me to the dining room. The lady of the house was there: a tall, full-figured, majestic, and at the same time simple and very warm woman. (She was no ordinary woman, and later I was able to call her "Mother.") From the very first meeting I felt a great sense of rapport.

Her brother-in-law P. Narutavicius (the father of the other young lady at Ginkunai) was at the dining table, and he was very talkative. When the lady of the house left, I ate supper and heard a lot of interesting stories about things that happened in Siauliai and Telsiai in 1905. I was really tired from the trip and from being nervous, and I was anxious to be shown to my room.

It was quite late the next morning when they called me to breakfast. When I got there, only the lady was there. The two high schoolers had already left for Siauliai, and the landlord was working in his study. While urging me to eat, the landlady asked me a little about my family and probed about various other things. I had to tell her everything, also tactfully. I was open about everything: my father's departure to America, my family's situation, my mother's problems. I didn't like telling them about my father, but I decided to bring up this unfortunate thing at the very beginning because I realized that sooner or later my new employers would find out about it. I left the dining room a little dismayed and even a little hurt, but later I realized that the lady needed to know these things about a total stranger for the sake of her family.

From then until lunch time (around 1 pm) I worked with the owner, who showed me the existing Ginkuna accounting system, with account books and documents. The cash register was turned over to me.

At one o'clock a gong rang as a call to lunch, a butler came to me and invited me to go to the dining table. In the dining room there were two impressive older women. They were mothers of the owner and his wife, by chance having arrived at the same time at Ginkunai, planning to stay for a few days. The students were not there; they usually only arrived around 3 pm. I was a little inhibited to be among educated people, chatting and getting to know me better. The owner and his wife sensed my hesitation and drew me out with specific questions, to bring me into the conversation. We talked about the revolution in South Russia. The owner's mother apparently heard that I recently arrived from South Russia and asked "Nu a Vy stoze?" (How are you?) The landlord answered for me that I had recently been released from prison. She smiled and insisted that I tell them about what happened in Gorlovko. It was clear that they were sympathetic with the rebellion.

The usual midday meal at Ginkunai was in three stages, all very carefully prepared. I was not used to a butler who dressed in a black coat and white gloves. He very formally, yet deftly and quietly, walked around the table, changing plates, serving food, and attending to the diners various ways.

I was encouraged to take a break until 3 pm. At that time I met the owner in the office and we worked until 7 pm that evening, going over accounting records. At 7 the dinner gong rang. I saw the owner's young daughter, in a school uniform, standing next to the lady in the dining room. She was Aleksandra Zubovaite. I saw for the first time the woman with whom I would spend the rest of my life and who made that life rich and beautiful. She had just returned from skating. Her cheeks were rosy and eyes very bright. She looked a bit tired. The outfit, and her hair worn pulled up, suited her. She shook my hand like a man and sat down next to her mother at the dining table. I sat on the opposite side.

Chapter 7

My life in Ginkunai had begun. It was just before 1907. The owner's daughter had just finished her 16th year and I was 22. I have been grateful to my parents-in-law my whole life, for their warmth and trust that surrounded me from the very first days of my job. For the three years I was at Ginkunai, I don't remember a single disagreement nor a single rebuke. They knew that I still hoped to continue my studies and saved my money for that. I think they paid me generously because of that. I had been shy with strangers my whole life and felt inadequate. Even at Ginkunai I was hesitant. I saw and felt that the owners were straight-forward and friendly toward me, but I still felt insecure with them.

The matron Sofija Zuboviene was especially good to me. I had had stomach trouble in prison. When I was released to Skaudvile, my sister looked after me and it got better. I didn't dare tell them that I needed a special diet at Ginkunai, and ate everything. It got worse, turning into a chronic condition. I didn't say anything for a long time but it was hard to hide it, as it got much worse and I stopped eating. Mrs. Zuboviene learned about my illness and tended to me, really nurturing me to health again. I was truly convinced of her extraordinary goodness.

In observing the life of my employers, I often saw them as models for social awareness and democratic ideals. They were respected by everyone and were worthy of that respect. Both of their children – son and daughter – grew up surrounded by tutors and teachers. Their first teacher was Tatjana Ferdinandovna Molas, who later married Dimitri Zubov and lived in Bubiai, where she was called Aunt Tania. There were three foreign language teachers, one after the other. The first, Mademoiselle Luiza, was a French teacher. After they learned French, the children learned German, and then English. The English tutor, Miss Jenny Sullivan, a young Irish girl, was there the longest time. Both of the young Zubov's were very open and friendly, not aloof, and sought to befriend me, but I felt hesitant and uneasy for a long time and avoided befriending them.

They loved music at Ginkunai. Mother and daughter played piano. The owner played a violin and his son, the cello. They often had concerts in the evening. The sincere, emotional and accessible music made a deep impression. I really wished I could play music with them. I started to learn to play the owner's old violin. In Siauliai there was a music teacher familiar with the composer Schuman. I started taking music lessons from him. Occasionally I was able to play simple melodies, but I could not read music and did not know the basic techniques of the violin. I wanted to learn and worked hard. I took lessons twice a week.

I did reach my goal and started playing with the Ginkunai ensemble. Having been exposed to the joys and pleasures of playing, I long dreamt of creating an ensemble after I left Ginkunai. I was able to realize that dream much later, as the administrator of Ginkunai farm, during the time of Lithuanian independence.

Only the Zubov daughter still lived at home, a student in upper classes of high school. Their son had finished high school and studied agriculture in Germany. There were three of us living in the main house: a secretary, who was a relative, an older nurse, and I. When I arrived in Ginkunai a niece also lived there – Zule Narutaviciute, and she went to high school with the daughter. Although there weren't many in residence, there were a lot of visitors – various relatives on the owner's side and on his wife's side. At that time the owner's mother was still living.

The owner's mother – a plump older woman with very controlled expressions – was good-looking and a little proud. Pride really suited her. She occasionally came to Ginkunai for a few weeks. She had a few rooms exclusively held for her. She was an unusual old lady: short, thin but agile, cheerful, of an affectionate and pleasant demeanor. If you ignored her high status (as the Countess Aleksandra Olsufjeva) and her highest class upbringing (a lady-in-waiting in the Czar's Palace), she was very ordinary, approachable, sweet, and pleasant with everyone. She was supporting a lot of young people, to whom she regularly distributed allowances from her trust funds. There were also older dependents who had been in service to the owner's parents.

The families of the owner's brother Dimitri and his sister Olga often visited Ginkunai. Dimitri owned land in the region of Bubiai, 13 kilometers from Siauliai. His sister had the Panusio farm in the district of Lygumai. Sometimes the owner's other sister Marija came to visit. She was married to Count Sergej Tolstoy, the son of the famous Russian writer. Count Sergej played piano perfectly. We had great concerts when he came to Ginkunai.

The large Bileviciai family – relatives on the wife's side – also came often.

Ginkunai was never lacking for visitors. The owners had yet many friends and acquaintances in the area around Siauliai. In the summer, two school friends of the son would stop for a few weeks. The son himself was seldom there, as he studied in Germany, and spent many of his summers there. The daughter spent winter and summer living at home. In the summer, we played croquette and tennis. I lost most of the time because she was more skilled.

After living in Ginkunai for a while, I found out that my close relative Ona Jokubauskaite was living in the household of Mr. Hiksa. She was the only daughter of my now-deceased uncle Jonas Jokubauskas, the same uncle who had offered to take me in in Liepoja and support me through high school. In Ginkunai it was said that Ona Jokubauskaite was very unassuming, serious, and played the piano very well. Absolutely certain that she was Jonas Jokubauskas' daughter, I went to Gubernija to the Hiksas to get to know my cousin. She wasn't home. I told the Hiksas who I was. They invited me to stay and wait for Niuta (her nickname), absolutely sure she would be delighted to see me. As soon as she got back, however, she wasn't very nice. She'd heard nothing about her cousin Jonas and was cool and officious toward me. Later, when her older brother told her about our kinship, she recognized me as a cousin and called me by name. In the meantime, I had found out that the Ginkunai owner's son Vladimir Zubov was courting Ona Jokubauskaite and intended to marry her. That happened. (Aunt Niuta and uncle Dziutkus.)

My employer treated me very well. He came to rely on me after he discovered I was very organized. It happened like this: every other year the whole family travelled to a foreign spa for a long time, leaving me in Ginkunai. The owner made me solely responsible for a small field of fodder crops. The field was neglected, overgrown with weeds, and the few growing beets looked ragged. I was informed about what to do to the field to revive the beet crop, but since I was completely ignorant about growing things, I did not completely understand what I needed to do. While the owner was gone, I found a book on growing beets in the library and studied it. It didn't take long. In a few days, I knew very well that beet need to be weeded, often hoed to loosen the dirt, and heavily fertilized with organic matter to add minerals. The field was not big – maybe 5 hectars. I got to work. The groundkeeper had been instructed to supply anything I needed. I got a few girls to help and we started weeding, fertilizing, and hoeing the field. It didn't go well with the girls' work. They were used to careless weeding and did not know how else to work. It took quite a bit to explain until they understood that the little weed you didn't pull today would be a big one in a few days. It was hard to get them used to the idea of hoeing around growing crops – that seemed completely wrong to them. After a few days of explaining and petering, they started to work well and fast. The beets started to come up. I was amazed how fast they responded to our work. When the owners returned from vacation, the beets were tall and so clear of weeds, I could offer a prize for finding one weed. The owner was very impressed and pleased when he saw the field. He said to me: "We've never had beets like these in Ginkunai." We went to the field often to take a look at the good crop. The beets were shown to visitors. This opportunity raised my cachet.

I was close to the owner's son – he had married my cousin Ona Jokubauskaite. Understandably this strengthened our ties.

For a long time my relationship with the daughter was formal and cool. We felt a rapport but we didn't show it. I didn't admit it to myself. The daughter, young and serious, understandably was raised traditionally and could not show me any affection. I was far from any idea we might have a family together and fiercely hid my feelings. It was hard to hide my feelings altogether – sometimes they showed when we danced or played games. It was only in the summer of my third year of work, when everyone knew that I would leave Ginkunai in the fall to study, that conditions were right and we did not hide our feelings for each other for a short while. This is how it happened: her father and mother left for a whole month's vacation in Germany, and their son, studying agriculture in Hale, had not yet arrived, and the secretary's position was vacant at the time. Her father asked his daughter to take over the secretary's work while he was abroad, since she had finished high school. That left just the two of us working in the office in Ginkunai. We worked in separate rooms but still the jobs of secretary and accountant required a lot of interaction and we could not avoid running into each other. We stopped avoiding each other and started dragging out our talks and spending more time with each other. We became friends, which had not happened before.

It didn't take long. The parents returned from abroad and sent their daughter and her grandmother to Jasnaja Poliana, to the Tolstoys.[1] A young man was also invited there, whom the grandmother had picked out as a husband for her granddaughter Aleksandra. The grandmother stayed with the Tolstoys several weeks. I have to point out that Leo Tolstoy was close to the grandmother – his son Sergei had married her sister-in-law Marija (Aleksandra's aunt). Jasnaja Poliana did not make a good impression. Aleksandra thought that Sofia Andrejevna (Tolstoy's wife) was very proud and aristocratic, which did not fit with the ideals of her husband. Aleksandra was surprised by the strangeness of Leo Tolstoy himself. He invited Aleksandra into his study (where he worked) and asked her where she studied and what she wanted to do in the future. Aleksandra told him she planned to study medicine. He tried to convince her that she did not need further study; that she was a country girl; born to raise children and take care of her household. He said Aleksandra did not need an education. She dared to disagree with the writer. Tolstoy got up, said, "I told you what I think," and left.

Aleksandra did not like the young man in question. When they returned from Jasnaja Poliana, she told her grandmother that the young man liked her

---

[1] Footnote by A. Fledzinskaite-Kasubiene: Her mother, Aleksandra Zubovaite, visited Poliana from childhood on. The families met nearly every summer. Her mother remembered sitting on Tolstoy's knee as he showed her how to scoop out a cucumber with a spoon.

initially. It was a good thing that she found them strange. She came back from Jasnaja Poliana a little disappointed. Tolstoy's halo was smaller.

I had to leave Ginkunai once my formal role was over, and I could start my studies. The owner's daughter could not start university in the school of medicine the same year after finishing high school because she was missing a high school course in Latin. She intended to study and pass an exam instead. Before she got to the exams she got very sick with a kidney infection. She spent nearly the whole winter in bed. Her entry into Berlin University was delayed until 1911.

Working in Ginkunai for three years had a significant effect on the rest of my life. That is, besides the fact that I met the girl for whom I hold dear a deep and lasting affection. Ginkunai gave me many spiritual and intellectual assets. On top of that, it gave me the means to realize a dream I'd had for a long time – to study. By working in Ginkunai, I had earned enough to last me a few years in the city.

Any thought of getting a degree had to be discarded. It was not possible to quit in the middle of a course and get somewhere. I had to be satisfied with something doable and more accessible. On the owner's advice, I entered the Advanced Business course in Petersburg (now Leningrad), with a broad legal and economic study program that could be completed in three years.

I started the courses in the fall of 1909. I recommended that K. Gruzdys, who was unemployed, replace me in Ginkunai.

Chapter 8

Advanced business course in Petersburg. Student life (study, cultural events, life style). Engagement.

When I arrived in Petersburg I found a room within a day, not far from my classes near Nevskio Boulevard. Course lectures started at 5 pm. The courses were taught by university professors who were busy at the university during the day. Evening lectures had a positive side – the whole day was free to visit museums and work in the library. I didn't know anyone in Petersburg except two women – K. Gruzdys' sisters. After I found my room and registered, I went to see the sisters. For the next three years, that was the only place I spent my occasional free time. Serious, but cheerful and nice, they were a perfect foil for my grouchy or gloomy moods. The younger one – Ona (now Mrs. Bugailiskiene) – especially liked to talk and laugh. Sometimes they gave me tea (supper) and sometimes they cooked up delicious cabbage with bacon my sister Juze had sent me. The cabbage was so good! I went to the theater and concerts with them. It was hard to get tickets to the theater, especially the Great Opera. There were long lines of mostly students at the theater box office starting early evening, trying to get tickets the next morning. The gallery seats (the worst seats) were cheap – 32 or 34 kopecs, but it was very hard to get them. Some people waited in line for hours for opera tickets, to see Saliapin or Smirnov. They brought blankets and sometimes pillows with them. It wasn't easy to get tickets to concerts either, but they required only a few hours in line. In those days there were two famous violinists who played in Petersburg a lot – J. Kubelyk and Guberman. They were very popular in Petersburg and both had large audiences turn out. Young people especially liked Guberman. After every concert, he would be surrounded by young people and pressed to play various short pieces. By that time the hall was empty and several dozen enthusiasts stood right by the stage, persistently insisting that he play new short pieces and loudly rewarding the encores.

The study program was a lot of work because in addition to attending lectures (up to 5 hours) every day, I had work on studies at home. I had some preparation in economics from working in the underground organization in Jenakijev. Accounting, which others found confusing and hard, was something I knew from practice. In general none of the coursework seemed hard to me because I was very interested and wanted it so badly.

There were several discussion sections with the courses, led by the professors themselves or by their assistants. From the very beginning I joined the economics group, which was led by a young, energetic, left-leaning professor Bernadski. He told us topics for our papers in advance and required serious preparation – reading a lot of material. There weren't many participating in the section – a number in the teens. We had to prepare two or three papers during the year. My first paper topic was "Syndication and Trust." The other "Legal Foundations of Consumer Cooperatives." Since the section was discussing cooperatives, a famous Russian cooperatives expert, Prof. Totomjanca came to our section meeting. He was a great enthusiast and expert on cooperatives. He participated in all the international congresses on cooperatives as the Russian representative.

At that time the literature on cooperatives in the Russian language was scant, so it was very interesting and necessary to hear the professor tell us about cooperatives in Western Europe, about congresses and views of cooperatives. The section organized excursions to cooperatives and their shops, to various factories, the stock market, and elsewhere.

I had to live very cheaply in order to make my money last. I rented rooms in a home for the care of seniors and ate at home in the morning and in the evening. The landlord gave me hot water and I bought tea, sugar, and bread. For breakfast and supper I had better things sometimes – my dear sisters sent me sausages, bacon, cheese, butter, cakes, and more. I ate dinner in the Polish cafeteria for students. It was the perfect cafeteria because the Poles formed a close group of friends. The food was very good, using good produce, and at the right low prices for students. For example, a big full bowl of good soup was 13 kopecs, a portion of jelly or stewed fruit, 4 kopecs. A nice, good bread was provided free on the side. Sometimes, when money was scarce, I would have just soup and bread for dinner. You could get a hearty dinner for 13 kopecs. I usually spent my summer vacation in Dabikine at the younger Zubov's house, straightening out their accounts for them. My sister Ona taught at the school in Dabikine, which was supported by the Zubovs. Many of the owner's relatives would visit Dabikine in the summer, to rest and pass the time.

My studies in Petersburg finished the summer of 1912. The diploma for my course of study automatically qualified me to enter the Commerce Academy in Berlin directly.

Once I left Ginkunais, I didn't have regular contact with the family. A few times over the summer, while I stayed with the younger Zubovs, I saw Aleksandra Zubovaite. We were alone only once over three years. That happened in Ginkunai. K. Gruzkys, now married (to Konarskaite) and living in Ginkunai, wrote and asked me to be sure to stop by on my way through Siauliai. After the holidays I travelled from Skaudvile to Petersburg, stopped at Siauliai and rode to Ginkunai. I didn't find the Gurzdys at home. They were gone to Suvartuva to visit Putvinskis. The owners at Ginkunai were home and received me very warmly. Their daughter had a kidney infection and lay in bed, set up in the library. That day both the owner and his wife had to leave and go to Bubiai. On leaving, the mother asked me to visit with her sick daughter, look after her, and read to her. We didn't manage to read very much. We talked about what we'd experienced and what we were planning to do. I was planning to continue my studies at the Berlin Commerce Academy. That evening we decided: if I succeeded in finishing the Handelhochschule (advanced school of commerce), and she, medicine or humanities, that we would get married. We separated only late that evening when the parents came back. The next day I left for Petersburg.

Only later I found out that right after I left, Aleksandra told her mother about our plans and got her blessing.

I was successful getting into Handelhochschule because I did well in my studies in Petersburg and because of V. Zubov's recommendation on my behalf.

Chapter 9

Our studies in Berlin. Work and living conditions. Trip to London. War is declared. Hurried return to Lithuania.

The Ginkunai owner's daughter also studied in Berlin. She studied medicine. When I arrived, she was already in her second year and living in Scharlotenburg. I rented a room on the opposite side of town so that I would not interfere with her studies and that I would not waste too much time either. On the contrary, the opposite happened. Travel took up a lot of time. We ate dinner at the same place, meeting every day, but that wasn't enough. When I got back from the academy, I rode to Scharlotenburg and got back at 11-12 pm at night. It took 40 minutes by train through the city, each way. I spent a lot of happy hours in Scharlotenburg. Sometimes I found a young lady Stencelyte there (now Doctor Stossinger, living in Karlsruhe), a roommate and an inseparable friend. They ate supper together, and often breakfast. They studied together, one reading, the other listening. Except they lived in separate rooms, near each other. We often all three drank tea and read the newspapers.

When I arrived, both girls were getting ready for exams. Social work took up a lot of their time. They had both joined a Polish social charity, which, among other things, specialized in teaching children to read and write Polish. There were a lot of Poles working in shops in Berlin. Their children went to German schools because there were not Polish schools in Berlin. Lacking a proper community, every factory organized a Polish school. They taught members of the charity in those schools. Once summer arrived, we started to take walks and excursions to the beautiful environs of Berlin. There wasn't much time left over for studies. We had decided that when we finished studies, we would get married.

While studying in Berlin, I went to London for a summer vacation and to get more exposure to English, which they taught in our academy, and, to see one of the biggest cities in the world. I decided to travel through Hamburg, to take a longer route, experience the sea, and to see the famous port.

I left on the express out of Berlin early in the morning and was in Hamburg in 9 hours. There were a lot of sights in the city – a zoological garden in which animals are not caged but roam free in the open air. The areas were separated by wide ditches, full of water. What really impressed me was the wide variety and number of wild animals. But the deer, elks, and other herbivorous animals – they would tremble in fear when they heard the lions roar.

The boat departed Hamburg late in the evening. It sailed for Henica, and from there we had to travel to London by train, because big boats cannot sail into London. It was quiet and pleasant sailing the boat up the Elbe River. Most of the passengers fell asleep in their cabins right away. However, after a few hours, the boat sailed into the North Sea, where a fierce storm was raging. It made our ship rock hard and tossed it in all directions. I was already asleep in my cabin. Suddenly I woke up and felt as if my head was sinking and my feet were going up in the air. My stomach turned very badly. When I realized that, I jumped out of bed, got dressed (falling hard all over the cabin), and, grabbing my hat and coat, dashed through the door into fresh air, went out on deck and rushed to throw up over the railing. The storm was really howling. It was so loud, that you couldn't talk on the deck. Suddenly the boat plunged down into an abyss and then roughly rose up. My heart was pounding as I held onto the railing, getting splashed with foam, so I went back inside. The rocking was considerably milder but the wind was still howling and tearing at my coat, and my heart was still pounding. I stayed in one place, hanging onto a railing, getting tired and cold after a few hours. In the evening the storm quieted down and it was possible to stand again. Hungry and tired, we ate breakfast and rested until noon. A fantastically beautiful evening made up for all of our discomforts.

When I arrived in London, I got sick. My feet started to hurt. I caught cold on the ship and my back nerves were inflamed. A doctor I consulted said I should lie down, take hot baths, and after that rub on various lotions. The rubbing was very irritating, but after a week I could walk again. While still in pain I sought out music, parks, and sights. On Sundays, I went to Catholic or protestant churches, so I could listen to the beautiful choral music. I was in London four weeks. The inflammation really kept me from getting to know the city better.

I returned through Antwerp, Brussels, and Koln, and stopped in each so I would know them a bit. In Koln, I visited a famous cathedral and ended up there during a worship service led by an archbishop, a few bishops, and a host of priests. The cathedral was decorated with fresh flower garlands and with a large area in front of the alter covered with carpets. An orchestra played without the organ, and two choirs sang.

The architecture of the Koln cathedral made a great impression on me. In Brussels I had visited a company where women hand-knit very fine sweaters. When I looked at the Koln gothic cathedral, I found similarities between a gothic style and the sweaters in Brussels.

Two years in Berlin passed by like a sweet and happy dream. There was finally time for a vacation in 1914. Both of my lady friends left for Lithuania. I had to stay in Berlin a few days longer because I had yet to finish some required assignments in the academy. A few days after the students left, I was eating dinner and read in a special newspaper edition that Germany had declared war on Russia. A conflict between the Russians and Germans was predicted, but not so fast and not so bad.

I called home to expedite getting my things together, so I could take the first train out of Germany, because once the war began the Russian-German border would be closed.

When the train arrived in Virbalis, the passengers were informed that the wagons headed for Russia would not continue on as usual, because it was dangerous and they might be captured there. The passengers were allowed to cross the border. But that posed a difficult problem: we could not take our things along without help. We would have to carry all of our things about two kilometers. Several of the passengers had very heavy luggage, and there were small children who had to be carried because they couldn't walk. We could not wait any longer because the border was going to close. So we proceeded on foot, helping each other. We didn't know what to expect in Kybartai. People we met along the way said nobody was left in Kybartai. But that night, empty rail cars arrived, and we gladly got out of Kybartai.

Chapter 10

Alina (Aleksandra's nickname) had been sick with kidney disease for several years. In the summer of 1914 her health got so bad that the doctor advised her to travel to Egypt as soon as possible, because the dry air relieved the disease. I was invited to come to Ginkunai from Skaudvile and was officially recognized as her intended. I was asked to take her to Egypt. The plan was exciting and everything was in place for the journey, but the war interfered, and we never went.

In the meantime, the Germans were pressing the Russians back and were approaching the boundary of Lithuania. Clearly it would not be long before Lithuania would be overtaken. We had to leave. Because of his daughter's poor health, the owner decided to head south. Her mother and I went with her.

That year the Zubov family was separated. The older parents were already separated and lived apart. The father was in Medemrode, and the mother in Smiltyne (where she had acquired some land next to the Dabikines estate). Mrs. S. Zuboviene left with her daughter and me, heading south. V. Zubovas headed north, to Medemrode. The son took his family to relatives in the area of Moscow. He himself volunteered to work in the Lower Region Union. (Funds for the Lower Region were maintained by a large organization, for the purpose of providing sanitation on the front lines.)

When we arrived in Crimea we intended to stay and recover in Jalta, but as we left Simferopel, we ran into the caretaker of a house in Simejizo, who offered to put us up. That was in the summer of 1915. That year, on March 29th, we were married. The Orthodox priest in Alupka who married us was very likeable and judging by what he said during the wedding ceremony, very wise. The witnesses were an engineer, Markun, who lived in Jalta at the time, and the church's watchman. There was no big celebration. Her mother (and now mine) served us a very nice dinner and a marzipan cake ordered from Talinn. We did not stay in Simejizo very long. I managed to get a job as a committee administrator in Jalta and we moved there to live. But we didn't stay together there very long either.

I was not drafted into the Russian army because I was the only son in my family. The Russians had a rule that, if you are an only son, you are excused from military service. They could not call me up. But big losses on the front lines could force the authorities to suspend the rule. I was safer working in a military establishment, and soon got the chance. My brother-in-law, the younger V. Zubov, asked me to come to Pskov and work in the Lower Region Union operation. It was hard to leave Jalta where we had a full and quiet life. We decided that I would go to Pskov by myself and my wife and her mother would stay in Jalta where the facilities to tend to kidney disease were better. Later they moved to Moscow and stayed there.

In Pskov, V. Zubov was the head of the Transportation Division. There were about a thousand horses under the oversight of the Division, mostly for the purpose of transportation, and a few hundred soldiers. Most of the horses were on the front. We held the reserves in Pskov and organized the transport of the wounded back from the front. They were brought to dressing stations, and from there moved behind the front. The Transportation Division was mainly concerned with horses and transportation vehicles, but also with the brigades on the front. We had to take care of field hospitals, disinfection sites, field bakeries, and other activities. To that end we often had to buy many horses, special and regular carriages, and harnesses.

I was offered the job of Deputy Director of the Division but after a few weeks was promoted to Director because V. Zubov was commissioned into the army and had to move to Riga. I wasn't the Transport Division Director for long either because I was assigned to take over the most difficult company Division – Supplies. It was a difficult job with lots of challenges – various products and materials were very hard to get, but they had to be supplied.

When I arrived in Pskov I found O. Gerasimov, the former Minister of Education, in the company leadership. I had to work with him for about two years. He was very capable and knowledgeable about administration. He was very demanding and strict, but fair, and tactful. He liked Lithuanians. I asked him why and he said that Lithuanians were more industrious and honest than others. He also explained his predisposition toward Lithuanians was due to his own Lithuanian blood – he'd been born there. In 1917, Gerrasimov was assigned to the Lower Region Union Central Office in Moscow and the writer and doctor Selpotjenskis replaced him. The same year, I was promoted to the Deputy position.

Working in the Lower Region Union gave me a chance to get involved in Lithuanian matters. Along with this job I was encouraged to head the "Grudas" Company. The company was created during the war. One of its founders was the senior V. Zubov. There were over a dozen Lithuanian families in Pskov. We were able to form a branch of "Grudas" quickly. Once the group started public works – aiding indigent Lithuanians, setting up schools for children, and so on, competition showed up. The Christian Democrats did not like a group over which they had no control, so they tried to break up our group various ways, and recruit our members to their club. We often met to discuss the group's needs and regular club business. Priests and other sympathizers came to these meetings too. Fierce arguments broke out. J. Glemza (later the "Pieno Centras" or Central Dairy Chief) worked not far from Pskov. I invited him to help me deal with the Christian Democrats. He very gladly attended our meetings and diffused various attempts to interfere.

The front was moving closer to Pskov. Our Division got the order to move north. It was hard to find a suitable place. We needed a lot of offices to accommodate about a hundred people, also a lot of space for storage, stables, and garages. We decided to start with Novgorod. It was about 250 kilometers from Pskov to Novgorod. I invited the State engineering unit to come with us. Early in the morning, we got into a nice 12-

cylinder Peugeot car and headed toward Novgorod. The road was in good shape but when we got to the town we discovered that the elevation of the bridge was significantly higher than the road. Our Peugeot was a very low car, well suited for good, even roads. We managed to cross the bridge in daytime, but when we returned to Pskov that night, the car got stuck on the bridge and we had a lot of trouble.

We didn't find suitable offices in Novgorod, so we redirected our attention to the east and found Rybinsk. Here, however, the work of our office was confounded. If we didn't go north, we lost a lot of resources – clinics, bath houses, transport, storage – and we didn't have any way to replace them. It was not easy to get to Rybinsk. A lot of units sent notice that they had run out of resources and the soldiers went back home. A big problem arose in Rybinsk too. The Soldiers and Workers' Party started to demand that all the Lower Region Union's resources be turned over to them immediately. I had to respond to the situation because the Director had long before gone to Moscow and didn't come back, because he saw trouble coming. I had nothing against cooperating with the Soldiers and Workers' Party (the Communist Party) because it was impossible to function under the new circumstances, with the front so far away and our communications with our units broken. But I could not hand over our resources without orders and approval from the Central Office in Moscow.

They did not respond to my telegram to Moscow. The Soldiers and Workers' Party started to threaten me with jail. One day I got into such a heated argument with a group of soldiers that they decided to "put me down" (throw me) from the third floor. I succeeded in calming them down, and cooler heads prevailed among them. We agreed that if I did not get approval from Moscow by 2 pm the next day, they would remove me from office and take all the resources for the Soldiers and Workers' Party. Fortunately, the evening of the same day I got the orders to turn over the resources, from the Central Office. I paid the manager's salaries. The next day we signed the transfer papers and completed the whole process.

I took the contracts and left for Moscow. In Moscow I found my wife and her mother. They had arrived from Jalta. They had spent quite a long time in Jalta and my wife had her health back. A huge brick house was bought in my wife's name in Jalta but before they could take ownership it was taken over by the state. We were all together again in Moscow. I started to look for work. I inquired with the managers of the Russian Consumer Cooperative's Association and got a reply that I could have a position as an instructor for cooperatives, if I passed certain exams. I had one and a half months to prepare for the exams. The exam was unusual: write a paper on an assigned topic and give a two hour talk in the large auditorium at Seniavsko University. The assigned topic was: "The History of Consumer Cooperatives." It did not seem very hard.

Already before passing the exam I was listed as a management employee in the Cooperatives Association. I could use the support that the association offered its members. I needed their help because of a food shortage in Moscow. We could get bread now and then, but it was bitter and poorly baked. The bread was made of oatmeal. We could get meat from time to time but it was horse meat. There were no potatoes, sugar, flour, butter, or other fats. The Cooperatives Association, which had separate products for residents, distributed all kinds of luxury produce to the managers. One time we got a whole goose.

After I passed the examination I was assigned to go to Arkhangelsk right away to take a 3-month course for managers of cooperatives. That meant yet another separation from my wife and her mother! We knew that citizens who had left the Baltic countries would be allowed to return to their homes. There were to be special trains organized for that purpose. Food was scarce in Moscow but as long as I worked in the Cooperatives Association we could subsist. If I were assigned to go to Archangelska, then I had to quit the association and things would get much worse. We decided that I would go to Archangelska and my two ladies would take the first train transport back to Lithuania.

While my wife and I still lived in Moscow we started to learn the Lithuanian language. We found a Mrs. J. Jablonskyte (now Petkeviciene) who gladly agreed to tutor us in Lithuanian. We both had a limited vocabulary and started to build a personal dictionary. We compiled several thousand entries.

Mission in Archangelsk. Impressions. Training for work. Meeting English people. Return to Lithuania. Settling in Siauliai.

I found a different world when I arrived in Archangelska: white and rye bread, butter, meat, eggs, and other products. People had enough except for things that were centrally produced in Russia – sugar, matches, tobacco and such. Everything was coming in without interference, even goods from outer regions. I didn't see a single brick house in the town. They were all wood, properly built using rough round logs. Many were two stories high. They were exceptionally neat and clean. As much as I can remember, all the streets were not paved. Sidewalks were boarded. The people were ordinary, warm, very productive, and much more cultured than residents of central Russia.

The Cooperatives Association people knew that I was coming. People were invited to the training from far away – about 300 people came in. They came from various educational backgrounds – from high school graduates to just having finished basic school. The trainees were ages from 15 years to 50. The classes were held in various rooms in the high school, and I found myself there. I got a very large, very bright room. There were no curtains on the windows and the room was light both day and night. It was summer, and the sun, having barely set on the horizon, rose again. All night it was light as day. White nights in the Baltics are very unnerving and made it hard to sleep.

While I was working there, a large English ship sailed into port, full of interesting goods. Soon we had products and goods from all over. You could smell English cigarettes in the street. Goods were offered to the State Cooperatives Association. They got in touch with the Moscow Central Cooperatives Association and bought out the whole shipment. The ship had a translator but he was not very strong in Russian, and, besides, he kept disappearing somewhere. Several times I was called to help the Association representatives communicate with the ship's administrators. I got to know a few Englishmen. English was not easy for me but since I was acting as interpreter and chatting with the English, they practically "grabbed" me. Several times they took me to the boat and treated me to great meals. They came to our classes to listen to Russian (or at least that's what they said), invited me to cafes, and so on. I later understood the motivation behind this behavior.

Only in Moscow did I learn that the English had set up a military base in Archangelsk. I finished my teaching and left for Moscow. The next night the English had occupied the city. Now I understood why they sent a ship to Archangelsk and what they needed from me.

After I arrived in Moscow I caught the next train transport to Lithuania.

I found my wife and her mother living very modestly on the Dabikine estate, in two small rooms co-opted from the housekeeper.

My wife and I went to Ginkunai thinking that the owner's daughter needed to reclaim her place. We asked to reclaim part of the house and rights. The Germans parted with token rights to crops and money but rigidly declined to give up any but a few rooms to us. "You have no reason to return to Ginkunai. You won't be living here anymore." One of the senior people explained, "Wir sind hier fur immer." ("We are here for good.") But after a few weeks they scuttled back to their fatherland.

We still couldn't settle into Ginkunai although the Germans had been driven out of Lithuania and the remaining roving troops defeated. The main house was a big mess and ravaged. It needed a lot of restoration which we could not afford immediately. The grounds and fields were stripped and ruined by the departing Germans – they took everything they could carry. Among animal stock only two non-working horses were left.

We settled into a two-story former manor house of the Zubov's near the park in the city. The house had belonged to the Gubernija estate. While living there, we had to survive the savagery of the Germans as they left Siauliai. I had to hide for about two weeks, as they were looking for me. The house we rented was later sold to the Education Ministry to be used as a college for teachers, so we had to move to a private apartment on Kursenai Street.

Our first son, Vytautas, was born in the house near the park, in 1919, June 10th. On August 3rd, 1920, while still in Siauliai, our daughter Zule was born. And January 10, 1923, our daughter Alyte was born in Ginkunai. In 1924 our son Jurgis was born, also in Ginkunai. We had moved back to Ginkunai from Siauliai only in 1922. With Jurgis' birth, our family was complete.

Chapter 12

My wife's parents and their personalities. Mother-in-law's influence on child rearing. V. Zubov's political views and public role. A Lithuanian school on the estate.

My wife's mother had separated from her husband and lived with us from 1915 on. When she returned to Lithuania from Russia, she bought a small place near her son's estate in Dabikene, in Smiltyne, where she stayed by herself from time to time. In the summers she took all of our children to Smiltyne with her, and took care of them. She put a lot of effort into raising them and educating them. Her great affection for her grandchildren helped us raise them to be healthy, both spiritually and physically. Her great intelligence, her tenderness, patience, and tolerance were a very good influence on the children. She was close to them, and she helped my wife and me create our happy life.

We were impressed how my mother-in-law, already quite advanced in age, quickly and clearly grasped that as part of the educated class in Lithuania we should speak Lithuanian at home and give up foreign languages. She readily and quickly fit in with us, learning to speak Lithuanian and infusing a Lithuanian culture into our family.

Her roots were in old Lithuanian noble families. Sofija was the oldest daughter raised in a prominent

Bilevicius family. She met V. Zubov while she was a student in the most advanced school in Petersburg, and married him. She was very interested in philosophy and pedagogy. She loved children and spent her whole life thinking about child-raising. She participated in various charities donating a lot of time to public works. She fostered and nurtured the Zubov's first schools which they founded and maintained, and in which everything was conducted in Lithuanian. She profoundly understood the meaning of Lithuanian nationalism that rose up at the beginning of the century, and heartily supported it. Living with us, she helped us create a Lithuanian family. It wasn't easy for her to hold her own and put up with her relatives – Poles, or with her husband's relatives – Russians. She never failed to support the path my wife and I chose, always supported us in trying for a purely Lithuanian family life. She lived to take care of others.

There is a Polish novel written by my mother-in-law – "Szenscie" ("Happiness"). Very few have seen the book; her husband Vladimir bought up all the copies.

My mother-in-law Sofija Zuboviene suddenly died in Ginkunai in 1932. She was completely healthy in the evening, packing her bags for a trip to Smiltyne the next day. We wanted to bury her near us, so she was buried in the Zuvininkai cemetery just on the outskirts of Ginkunai. We could see her grave and cross from the veranda in Ginkunai.

My wife's father Vladimiras Zubovas was Nikolai Zubov's oldest son. He finished high school in Siauliai and university in Petersburg. While still in high school he belonged to illegal organizations and was very active in them. In the university he got close to progressive Poles and the PPS – the red Polish socialist party. He was a progressive his whole life and close to leftist political parties. He had ongoing ties with the German Social Democrats and donated considerable sums of money to their cause. He approved of the revolutionary movement in Russia, but apparently he did not have ties with the revolutionaries. Given the opportunity, he gladly helped various revolutionaries, for example, he helped Kapsukas flee to Western Europe, and helped hide the returning Lithuanians at the Medemrode farm. He supported the Lithuanian nationalist movement, organizing gatherings of Lithuanians, and participated in them. He was active in matters of education policy. He was one of the first to found Lithuanian schools, running them directly himself. The schools were supplied with buildings, fuel, and electricity. The salaries of the teachers, and even the watchmen, were paid out of the estate's budget. He found teachers Jadvyga Juskeviciute, Stanislova Landsbergyte and others to teach and take care of educational matters. My sister Ona taught for a long time in the school at Dabikene. There were five Lithuanian schools maintained by the Zubovs: Ginkunai, Naisiai, Seksciai, Medemrode, and Dabikine.

Besides investing a lot in schools, they stood out in serving public interests. They supported disadvantaged students. They directly helped poor families, the disabled, school children, and others.

V. Zubov was hugely fond of music. We had many great evening concerts. The father played violin, most often accompanied by his daughter and sometimes his wife. He did not have great technique but his playing was expressive and moving. Those evenings prompted me to study music. The father was good-humored and playful –

he liked to play tricks on people, some of them not so funny.

When he lived in his own farm, Medemrode, he visited us occasionally, although his health precluded frequent trips. Since we had a car, we visited him often and socialized for the day. He died in 1932. He was buried in the old cemetery near the Medemrode estate.

Chapter 13

The Zubov land holdings and their distribution through inheritance from Nikolaj Zubov.

After Nikolaj Zubov, died his legacy of large areas of land, farms, and forest were distributed.

To his wife, Aleksandra Vasiljevna, he granted the Gubernija estate with an existing beer brewery. From long past that part of the Nikolaj Zubov's property was known as the "economy of Siauliai" and that label persisted until land reforms.

Nikolaj gave his older son Vladimir the Ginkunai estate complex, to which belonged Ginkunai, Naisiai, Dimaiciai, Karvazai, Seksciai and Aliniske, and besides that, a large expanse of forest at Lova and Gervinai.

To his other son Dimitri he gave the Bubiai estate complex with several small residences and a large area of forest.

He gave his daughter Olga (Olsufjeva) the Pamusis estate near Lygumai.

No estate went to his second daughter Marija who married Sergej Tolstoy, because apparently she had received a dowry in cash.

Thus at the beginning of the 20th Century the Zubovs managed a large area of land. It was managed in three sections: Ginkunai, Medemrode, and Dabikine. Overall the land with the forest approaches 4000 hectars.

V. Zubov lived in Ginkunai and managed the cluster of estates himself. Medemrode and Dabikine estate groups were later acquired from the Vilnius Land Bank Trust, which bought these from a German baron when he went bankrupt. The fields were managed by a senior administrator who lived on the Medemrode farm.

Both groups had several farms – a total, it seems, of 12 residences. Their particular area of land was about 2500 hectars. They were not cultivated quite as intensively as the Ginkunai complex because they did not have an inventory.

V. Zubov was a progressive and orderly caretaker, with about 16 farms to administer, especially Ginkunai, and he could be considered a model for proper caretaking. In those times the culture of land management was not at a very high level. Farms were impoverished. People said, "The farmers ride horses and the goats work the land." It was different with Zubov's farms – the land was intensively and closely worked, with well-maintained buildings, high yields, well-fed, beautiful animals, and well-paid workers. The salaries to workers were considerably higher than those on other estates.

There was a beautiful herd of cattle in Ginkunai. When he started farming, V. Zubov decided to raise purebred "Fiunai" breed of cows. In order to do that he imported some cows and a bull from Denmark. Later more bulls were imported from Denmark. Several new strains of cattle were raised in Lithuania drawing on the purebred herd in Ginkunai. Milk from Ginkunai was sold in bottles, getting packed on wagons headed for Siauliai twice a day. Ginkunai also initiated the export of butter. A brand "Birute" was created through a joint effort of several large farms, and the butter was exported to Denmark.

Since Aleksandra's parents were separated, the ownership of the land was divided. The father kept Medemrode. It passed to his second wife after his death (Vera Usakova-Bielskiene-Zuboviene). The Ginkunai complex was given to his daughter Aleksandra. The Dabikine estate had been given to his youngest son (Uncle Dziutkus – Vladimir) when he married. Aleksandra's mother refused the share she was due by law.

Chapter 14

As I mentioned before, five farms belong to Ginkunai estate: Naisiai, Dimaiciai, Seksciai, Karvazai, and Aliniske. After the war these farms were left in a mess. When the Germans left, the farms were run by worker's teams comprised of three people. The teams' position was unenviable – the farms were completely bare. No live animals, no equipment, and the barns were empty. The workers called on us to tell them what to do. It was suggested that we all get together and jointly talk about the condition of the farms. The meeting took place at our house in Siauliai on the earliest Sunday. In the discussions, we learned that there was a glimmer of hope – a few Ginkunai cows were with our neighbors and with workers, and some harvesting equipment turned up.

At the meeting we decided to create a common group that would oversee farm activities that affected everyone. The governing body would have six members. We chose a Director. I was asked to be the Secretary. The group was to meet every Sunday at our house in Siauliai. The workers well understood the catastrophic state of our farms and showed a lot of sense. We started to repair and rebuild.

After the land reform laws were passed we were left with just the Ginkunai farm to manage, since the others were assumed by the State Land Trust. It was not easy to tend to the Ginkunai farm as it was tended before the war under the progressive and experienced V. Zubov Senior. The workers were very capable and used to a certain system, and used to order. I was not knowledgeable about farming. My prior work at Ginkunai did not prepare me for the management of the land. I just started to get interested. I learned a lot and understood a lot walking around the fields with the owner, but I was missing a lot in terms of assuming full responsibility. V. Zubov, knowing exactly how to help me, recommended a good, experienced overseer - -a German. Under him as a grounds keeper was an energetic and honest Lithuanian from the Klaipeda region. However, we did not like their approach, and besides, to really direct the management, I had to have a good understanding of farming myself. I surrounded myself with specialized books and started learning the trade of farming. I used every opportunity to consult with agricultural experts. The land management professors at Dotnuva helped me a lot when I consulted them about various farming questions. Soon I felt stronger and we did not need an expert general overseer.

We shared the work on the farm. My wife took over keeping the house, the garden, and the cow shed. It was a hard and unpleasant job. She had to get up about 4 am in the morning to supervise the milking of cows. There was no break for the holidays. She had to supervise milking, distributing the milk, feeding cows and calves, providing water, cleaning up, and tending to their health. Milking cows in the morning was especially hard as you had to stand in the shed for two to three hours. My wife knew how to tend to their health and enjoyed it. She got that satisfaction from her father who was interested in veterinary medicine and healed the animals. His daughter assisted him in performing various operations.

My wife also liked to tend to people. She knew a lot from three years in medical school. She was good at diagnosing illnesses not only by examining the patient but by using her intuition, from which she got excellent diagnoses. The premises of democracy were deeply embedded in Aleksandra. From childhood through her entire life she treated the poor and rich alike, as well as workers and landowners. Her sympathies lay more with those who had less, over the rich. When she was little she played with the worker's children. Later when some of them had children they would come to Ginkunai to remember good times from their childhood.

Music filled our free time. While working at Ginkunai I started to learn to play the violin. I took lessons from a music teacher who was a good violinist for two years in Berlin. The violinist Jurkevicius lived in Siauliai and I studied with him. Both of our sons were his students. When I got to know Jurkevicius better, we got the idea to start an ensemble. The first one included my wife (piano), Jurkevicius (violin), Petras Armonas (cello), Jurkevicius' student Stasys Gabrijolavicius (alto) and me (violin). Later as I improved, S. Gabrijolavicius played second violin, and I played alto. We gathered at Ginkunai every Sunday and played a couple of hours. We played the easier quartets and quintets. It was a serious repertoire from the very beginning. Our playing wasn't perfect because we were inexperienced musicians. In spite of that, we really enjoyed those hours.

After we moved to Ginkunai I had to go to Siauliai every day because I had regular work with the cooperative there. Mornings and evenings I worked on the farm, and during the day, for the cooperatives. I had even more than that, working with other organizations, for example, the Department of Land and Farms, the Association for Cattle Management (those producers who raise new breeds of cattle), Pig Growers, Seed Producers, the Sugar Producers Friendship, New Farmers Society, and banks: the Commission for Inspection of State Banks, and the Board of the Land Bank. In addition, I often had to go to Kaunas for various projects, invited by the government, and travel abroad for certain national and cooperative business. It was a great period of my life – about twenty years. I was happily involved in a lot of public business, and I could contribute and be useful.

There wasn't a year during which I did not have to go abroad several times. I travelled to England, Sweden, Denmark, Germany, and the Netherlands, not to mention nearby countries – Latvia, Estonia. It was a great pleasure to travel so much. The reasons varied: buying new breeds, negotiationing with firms, participating in conferences (mostly on cooperatives), and so on. Sometimes I visited countries on the way just to see them and people there (Norwegian fjords, cities in Belgium and the like).

To buy new breeds of animals I had to drive a car around the countryside. For example, to buy new breeds of sheep and goats and to facilitate reproduction, I had to drive several hundred kilometers to south Sweden.

I was able to go to Rome. I was a delegate to the International Congress on Land Management. The trip was interesting because I had already travelled a lot in the north but never in the south. On the way I stopped in Dresden, where I went to famous museums, although I couldn't see a lot in one day.

I was in Rome a whole week. I spent several hours attending the conference during the day, which left time to see the sights in the ancient city. The remains of the old civilization were especially impressive. I felt totally insignificant within the catacombs. It was strange to walk on the same pavement in Northern Italy that Roman legionaries had trod. The aqueducts were a great example – they supplied the city with fresh spring water for several hundred years. It was a tremendous feeling to enter the Coliseum. And the museums! There were so many historical things! The Vatican, churches, Saint Peter's and Paul Cathedrals, the Vatican museum. I found a map of Lithuania at the time of Vytautas the Great there. They could not say who provided the map.

We lived to see wonderful results from the love and devotion my wife and I put into our work. Ginkunai stood out for its high harvest yields and production of livestock. Every morning and afternoon, milk was sold from our wagons in Siauliai. The wagon was driven all over town. We sold up to 500 liters of milk a day. New breeds of bulls, raised carefully to yearlings, were sold at the age of 1.5 years for high prices. Our new breeds were imported from Denmark. We paid up to 10,000 Litas for them. Our crop seeds were often ordered from the best farms in Sweden. The seed from imported crops were sold to farms all over the country and we used it ourselves.

I remember that the original oat seed "Golden Rain" ("Goldenregen") 250 kg bought in Sweden brought a ten-fold crop. We raised sugar beets – grown in four hectar plots and turned the whole yield over to the Sugar Producers Association, getting back about 30,000 Litas. The farm usually had up to 130 livestock, of which 90 were milking cows.

Once we finished fixing up Ginkunai, we had some surplus funds and acquired another farm near the town of Telsiai (Gaudikaiciai). Over a few years we built some buildings, restored the farm, and increased crop production. We bought about 30 milking cows. The new farm started to give us a great income. The last year we ran the farm it yielded about 20,000 Litas in pure profit.

It is fair to say that managing a farm is not without problems, lots of crises, and disappointments. The building that housed workers in Ginkunai burned down. We built 8 new apartments, each with a great-room, a separate kitchen, and generous storage. We were successful in farming. Our relationship with workers was always good because we were cordial. We provided them with good incomes and the hours were reasonable. They valued these conditions and worked conscientiously. They were self-disciplined, and, it appears, resisted the agitators from Siauliai, who often visited the farm to leave propaganda. We knew about every visit. As soon as they started to approach the workers (mostly women), we were notified – "They are here." We did not interfere. They raised the worker's consciousness of issues, and that could not hurt the farm.

Life in general on the farm was greatly helped by the warm presence of the teacher Liuda Tomkyte (now

Ceponiene), who taught at Ginkunai many years. She was very sociable and popular and earned respect not just among people on the farm but far around it too.

In describing life in Ginkunai, I have not mentioned many community services. This wide and rich area of work took up a lot of time but gave us a lot of moral satisfaction and a sense of reward. During the whole time from the independence of Lithuania until the start of the Second World War, we were busy in the community. This did not interfere with our tending to farm business, and made our lives all the more worthwhile and greatly interesting during this period of twenty years.

Chapter 15

The country's economic and public situation after the war. The Consumers Community Association in the Siauliai region. Courses on cooperatives, local government, and accounting. "Sietynas" newspaper. Dealing with issues of trade and export. Objectives of "Gamintojas." Activities at "Pienocentras" or Dairy Center. The Association for Livestock Breeding and Control. Export of grain, flaxseed, eggs, and flax. The work of educating the rural population.

The state of the country after the first World War was a deplorable poverty. The country essentially did not have any industry. There were a few wind mills. The country was lacking civil servants. There were a few functioning lumber mills. One or two beer or alcohol breweries. That's all. And even these were destroyed by the Germans. The nation's farms were weak and primitive during the war and even so, managed to feed the populace. After the war, they were left without livestock, seed, tools, and even without bread. The Germans took over the large farms (whose owners had fled) and left them ruined. They took absolutely all the produce from the small farmers. Not only animals and harvest, but every egg, piece of ham, butter, bite of bread – all were plundered from the farmers. Units of German soldiers walked through the farms, conducted searches, and confiscated produce from the farmers and sent them to Germany, to their starving families.

The market was completely ruined. Farms had nothing to sell and thus no money with which to buy anything, and there was nothing to buy. There was no salt, kerosene, sugar, not to mention iron or metal goods. A temporary government was preparing land reform laws and elections to the Member Parliament. They had put a lot of effort into making it possible to recover the farm land, to address the most critical issues, and recover from the damage that had been done. Having shaken off foreign occupation and feeling free in an independent country, heated and lively spirits worked and stimulated a whole people.

There was work to be done in Siauliai as well. I had to revive the cooperatives, get them going again, and provide goods as well as personnel. The Consumers Union was moribund. It was completely broke having been disbanded, because there was no market, most of the cooperative accounts were not maintained, and there was no one to maintain them.

A group of professionals in Siauliai got together (P. Bugailiskis, K. Venclauskis, S. Lukauskis, Father J. Jasinskis, J. Naujalis). We decided to take the initiative and establish a Chamber of Commerce. There were no cooperative associations in Lithuania yet. One association would work for the whole country, and it should be based in Kaunas. However, the people in Kaunas still had not thought about setting up a Chamber at that time. We had to get one established quickly because the Americans were offering food products and were only interested in selling wholesale to a large organization. We decided not to wait for Kaunas District and to establish the Chamber in Siauliai, but not for all of Lithuania – just for Siauliai district alone. The idea that germinated in Siauliai was widely supported in the Consumers Association, and in 1919 the first Siauliai-region Chamber of Commerce was established. Through the association, members were provided wih kerosene, sugar, fat, and other American merchandise. Little by little scarcity in the market was alleviated.

The other big agenda was to recruit people. Literate people, let alone those who understood accounting, were very scarce. We had to recruit them quickly. We decided to provide short courses. In 1920, we conducted the first "Course on Cooperatives, Local Government, and Accounting." We accepted into the course good students who could read and write, with a preference for members or local government servants. A lot of people wanted to take the course. We chose appropriately and closed the enrollment at 30 people. I got to work with the trainees. The duration of the course was limited to about four months, so the trainees had to be pressured. As soon as I finished with the first group, I started with a second, as apparently there was great demand from people who needed it. They came from far districts. It was typical that the postal service, short on workers who knew Morse code, appealed to our Association to prepare their workers. The Society did not refuse even this job. Engineer V. Kurkauskas was recruited to develop a course in telegraphy. Shortly after the Society's course it was possible to straighten out the Chamber members' accounts.

Another priority for the Chamber leaders was publishing periodicals. There were a lot of issues to discuss that were local issues which the central newspapers did not address. There were issues in the work of the cooperatives that people needed to have explained. We decided to issue a regular newspaper ("Sietynas"). The editor and publisher was the popular P. Bugailiskis, who gave the publication a lot of time and attention.

Little by little as the Chamber of Commerce cleaned up the region and we started to think about arranging to export our farm produce. After the war, the export of farm products was reactivated. It was again in the hands of foreign merchants. The Lithuanian language was foreign to them, and even more important, they had a poor understanding of the interests of Lithuanian farmers.

Flax, eggs, butter and other farm products started to be exported as much as before the war. Linen, if not carefully and specially prepared, had a bad reputation abroad and therefore got the lowest prices. A handful of flax merchants monopolized the whole market and dictated prices to the producers. Butter bought in the market was a mix of good and bad quality, sometimes unintentionally, to be fair, and would be sold at the prices of the lowest quality. Because our eggs were not inspected and sorted, they were totally unacceptable to the English market. Lithuanian eggs, by the time they were shipped, turned out to be old, if not hatched. Buyers bought Lithuanian eggs, transported them to Riga, sorted them out, packed up the best, and exported them to London as produce from Latvia. They did the same with flax. Most of the eggs bought in the market were sold at low prices in Germany. Grain that was unsorted and not cleaned was also saleable to the Germans, who liked everything, because they were hungry and looked for the best prices. That's how dysfunctional our export system was. Better produce was sent abroad mixed with the bad, and so we got the lowest prices, because they were rated as the lowest on the market.

We went to England to talk about the potential of export from Lithuania. They advised us that at that time, exports from Lithuanian markets were not allowed to be sold in London. If we wanted to find a market there, we had to improve our export products and meet London's market standards.

What did we have to do to improve our exports? A lot: we had to find and train specialists in every type of produce, and we needed capital. For example, it was clear that we could not obtain high quality butter from butter sold in the markets, for various reasons. If we wanted butter suitable for export, then we had to modernize the country's dairies, which could be supplied with farm milk and then export products on a large scale.

The same was true of grain exports. Grain export was impossible without grain elevators, where grain could be dried out, separated from chaff, and sorted. It would take a big investment to build elevators and dairies and the government did not have the funds. There weren't people in the country who knew how to put together this scale of needed investment capital. Only the government, in collaboration with the public, could properly create an organization for the export of products. There were no private initiatives that could lead to an export organization in the country, and they were not welcomed. We could not leave the export of farm products disorganized because it was unprofitable. There were few foreigners interested in buying Lithuanian products.

The government did not take the initiative to set up exports but they also did not interfere with the cooperative's doing it. The Kaunas Cooperative didn't show interest in exports. Siauliai thus took the first steps.

Farmers could set up exports and succeed because they had provincial agents and business ties abroad. A farmer's partnership could execute these arrangements, united as a group. In 1922, the Food Producers' Association "Gamintojas" was organized in Siauliai.

It was clear that the establishment of Gamintojas could not solve all the export needs, and they didn't try. Gamintojas would take care of more modest goals: form an organization and carry out exporting that met world standards, remove unproductive middlemen in the export process, and develop the needed experts.

Once Gamintojas was established, our first concern was to take care of farmers' needs and new development. Several cooperative dairies were re-invigorated as they had survived from before the war. However, our efforts to set up dairies fell apart, because the government decided to establish a dairy farmer's co-op to build modern dairies, and to take charge of groups that organized the export of butter. It was to be called "Pienocentras" or "Dairy Center" and it was to buy up milk from the whole country. It was a very large and important step. The organization was capable of starting up milk exports the right way and to build expertise. They started to export quality butter. The butter was easily sold in London. The quality of the butter started to improve through a slow, easy but systematic process. All milk product exporting went through the hands of a state institution – the middle men were eliminated. The results of these changes were very quickly realized.

The head of the "Pienocentras" was the energetic and popular Jonas Glemza. His office carried out a broad agenda. Its charge was to promote milk production through partnerships, develop expert leaders. It organized quality oversight, control, and guidance. It forced farmers to improve quality and increase production. The "Pienocentras"built a nice building in Kaunas, in which, among other things, a very popular Lithuanian restaurant was opened. The public could eat breakfast, lunch, and dinner cheaply. Patrons appreciated the clean, fast service and good country cooking – they often had to wait in line to get in.

The milk production partnership was closely associated with another organization concerned with raising livestock – the Association of Inspectors. Inspectors had easy access to farms and soon served throughout the country. Every group had a specialist in quality control. They helped their members improve cow fodder, the raising of calves, increasing the variety of livestock. They helped their members utilize farm-raised cow feed more efficiently and were looking after the quality of milk. They were very good advisors to farmers on aspects of milk production.

Another related group was the Cattle Growers Association, concentrated exclusively on cattle breeding: the Dutch, Danish, and local. These three cattle growers' groups had a big impact on our livestock. They quickly increased our production of milk and separated cows into types by their quality and production. There was no longer a place for middle men in the production of milk and export of milk products. The production of butter and cheese was in the hands of processing partners, and export was in the hands of the collective "Pienocentras." Both production and export were collectivized, using effective methods. All that remained was to expand and improve them.

A similar principle was applied to export of eggs and cattle. Hogs, sheep, and goats (and later birds) were sent to three modern slaughterhouses (Kaunas, Siauliai, and Panevezis). The meat was exported to England and other countries. Especially the number and quality of pigs increased. The Pig Growers Group watched over pig raising. There was also a Sheep Growers group. In this way too there was no longer room for middlemen in the sale and export of livestock.

There were three important products whose export was not controlled: grains and flaxseed, eggs, and flax.

Once Gamintojas was in operation, one of its first concerns and efforts was to build modern grain elevators that were needed not only for the export of grain and flaxseed, but to produce more grain seed and distribute it more effectively. The Gamintojas members met twice on the question of building grain elevators and made decisions accordingly, directed to the Government, petitioning urgently that they build modern elevators and allow farmers' co-ops to use them. Quickly the Government decided to build elevators in Kaunas and Siauliai. To oversee the building of the elevator in Kaunas and open it for use, the Kaunas farmers' association was assigned. In Siauliai, Gamintojas ordered machines for one elevator from England and the other from Sweden.

By building the elevators and turning them over to the oversight of the cooperative, in essence, the export of grain and flaxseed became collectivized. Middlemen again had no place here. We should recognize that at that time, the grain produced was poor quality. It was hard to set up an effective export for it separately. Besides, there was not much spare grain to export – harvests were not adequate yet. Later, when farm cultivation improved, and the yield was larger, there was still not a lot to export because we started raising hogs intensively and used a lot of grain as feed for livestock.

It was hard to organize the export of eggs and flax. Private buyers, exclusively foreigners, monopolized the flax market and ran it badly and without scruple. When they bought linen from the farmers, they paid the same for good flax as for the lowest quality, thereby not compensating farmers for the higher quality product. Cleaning of flax was not rewarded – there was no difference in price. They had to work hard to find buyers so they could sell flax at all, and the buyers sometimes found rocks inside the bundles (to inflate the weight). Lithuanian flax had the worst reputation abroad for flax. Nobody wanted to buy it, and they paid the lowest prices.

It was similar in the case of exporting eggs. Private egg buyers bought from local markets. They did not check them for freshness. Lithuanians did not know about checking eggs based on transparency and sorting them by size. The eggs bought in local markets were packed in boxes and transported to Germany, where they bought everything, or to Latvia. There they were checked and sorted and the select ones were sent out as Latvian products to England, where the price of eggs was higher. Lithuanians did not have an export relationship with England because they had such a bad reputation. Our buyers bought all of them for the same price, not according to weight, and paid the same for large and small, the same prices for fresh and aged. Understandably, this discouraged the countryside chicken farms from working on improvement. The Gamintojas leaders decided to organize the flax and egg exports. In order to do that they needed the right experts in quality control.

There was only one option: to invite experts from West Europe and ask them to train Lithuanian people. Clearly, it would raise costs to hire foreign experts, but Gamintojas leaders were firmly decided to accomplish the task or not take it on at all.

Matters regarding flax and egg exports were directed to the Government through general memoranda. The Government was asked to help Gamintojas financially, through a subsidy, for a limited time, for every egg exported and for every unit of flax (50 kg.). Such a subsidy would give the cooperative the ability to get lower prices for products, and that way, stimulate an increase in flax and egg production. The Government declined to support export, apparently not understanding the principle. Later, the "Pienocentras" took over the export of eggs, and the Government agreed to subsidize every egg sold abroad 2 or 3 cents each.

The leadership of Gamintojas appealed to Danish representatives to recommend experts on egg or flax export.

Besides specialists, the operation of the export required significant capital and for that we tried to appeal to foreign countries. The London British Overseas Bank agreed to finance flax and egg exports on the condition that the credit be underwritten by the Lithuanian State Bank. Exports began in 1923. The first shipments of eggs and flax to England went smoothly and without loss. Exporting grew and expanded. The wall was broken, and a wide opportunity opened. The cooperative was buying eggs not by the unit but according to weight and the price was set by kilograms and not by count. All the eggs were inspected and sorted by size.

Gamintojas exported flaxs and eggs until 1926, when it was forced to stop operations because of losses related to flax export. The price of flax had gotten very high in the world market and suddenly fell. With a big flax inventory we had to accept low prices. Gamintojas was not able to cover losses with its own capital. Flax export was unprofitable for two reasons: intense competition from purchase of flax by private buyers and the failure to sell large stocks of flax. The Government Bank had to cover Gamintojas losses.

Gamintojas was founded to create opportunities for producers in the county and in the world market, and to develop export specialists. We had reached those goals. Gamintojas set up export of eggs and flax. Lithuanian farmers reached the market without middlemen and were able to obtain the confidence and trust of the market, and a good name. There were experts in the countryside who could independently continue the export operations.

The "Pienocentras" took over the whole egg export operation of Gamintojas and successfully continued it. "Lietukis" (the Lithuanian common partnership group) took over flax sales but they were not very interested in the operation and did not really use our experts after they took over. The biggest piece of flax exports stayed in the hands of buyers. Still, since the cooperatives also bought flax, this forced the buyers to pay higher prices and to meet export standards for exported flax.

Besides putting export activity in place, Gamintojas made other contributions to farming. The cooperative was asked to manage two large estates – Gruzdziai and Sepkaiciai. The estates were in awful condition. The fields were neglected, weeds overgrown, buildings wrecked but standing, no horses and herds, the equipment had been taken away by the Germans or sold. There were a handful of worker's families still there, waiting for the farm to be parceled out. The people were hungry. They needed work. The cows needed fodder, potatoes and vegetables had to be planted. The people were happy to get grain. The farm had a difficult and unpleasant challenge. Gamintojas was able to fix up the farms, repair the worker's cottages, work the fields, and obtain a rather good harvest. The estate manor houses were used for cultural events. What was the Naryskin mansion was now turned into a farming school, with courses for milk farmers and inspectors. The farms were full of young people, hungry for new ideas. A lot of resources went into the farms, but recovery was slow.

Gamintojas wanted to help farmers as fast as possible and organized travelling courses. Three groups of agriculture lecturers were formed. They travelled to farms and gatherings and gave a series of lectures. The mobile training was organized in Siauliai, Muzeikiai and Telsiai regions.

Cooperation was an evolutionary path toward improving people's lives, among people in the cooperatives movement. It was a means to a better spiritual and material life. In order to do that, productivity had to increase too. It had to be nationalized and collectivized, to eliminate social dependency. It was not hard to achieve that in our country.

The most beautiful and rewarding years of my life were spent at Ginkunai. My wife and I worked together in total agreement and mutuality. Our children grew up and matured there.

When Ginkunai was appropriated by the Land Trust, my wife stayed and got a position in the office. When she was warned of the threat of getting deported, she joined me in Kaunas. There she succeeded in getting an accounting position in the Panemune hospital. Later when we settled into Putvinskio Street, there was no question of taking another job – she had to run our household. There were four of us: my wife, Alyte, Jurgis, and I. The children went to school and I had a job. Soon after that the Germans were driven out of the country. After that I worked in Trapai and we lived in Skaudvile.

When the office moved to Silgaliai, we settled there and both my wife and I worked there. After Silgaliai we ended up at the nursery in Trapai and worked there for three years, my wife in the billing office and I in accounting. When my health got worse, I gave up the job in the nursery and returned to Skaudvile. I was not able to get a job in the small town. My wife was able to get an accounting job in the Education Department.

Skaudvile

1958-1959

1885	Born August 12 in Skaudvile.
1889	Father abandons family & emigrates to U.S.A. when JF is 4 years old.
1891	Wife Aleksandra Zubovaite is born.
1898	Finishes primary school at age 13. Gets first job as tutor.
1900	Older sister takes job near Petersburg so he can attend school. Works as tutor in Ringuvenai.
1901	Older brother dies.
1903	Mother dies. Goes to Jenakijev to live with sister. Gets work in factory as bookkeeper.
1905	General strike among factory workers. Loses job. Participates in revolution/armed rebellion & spends time in prison (1-2 years?).
1907	Returns to Skaudvile out of prison. Begins working at Ginkunai as a bookkeeper (22 years old).
1909	Leaves Ginkunai after three years for higher education in Petersburg.
1912	Finishes studies in St. Petersburg in the summer. Goes to Berlin where Aleksandra has already been one year. Trip to London.
1914	Evacuation from Berlin as Germany declares war on Russia. Family separates (father to Medemrode; mother to Smityne; brother-in-law to Moscow area).
1914	*WW I begins in August; Germany declares war on Russia.*
1915	Marries Aleksandra Zubovaite at age 30. Mother-in-law joins household.
1917	Works on supplies for Russian army. Family adopts the Lithuanian language at home.

1918	Lives in Moscow, as instructor in Russian consumer cooperative association. Returns to Ginkunai.
1918	*WWI ends in Oct-Nov.*
1919	Returns to Siauliai; Initiates Siauliai chamber of commerce. Son Vytautas is born June 10th.
1920	Daughter Zule (Sofija) is born August 3rd. Teaches courses on cooperatives. Post-war Conditions are very bad.
1920	*Lithuania is recognized as independent.*
1922	Moves from Siauliai to Ginkunai. Organizes Food Producer's Association "Gamintojas" with others
1923	Daughter Alyte (Aleksandra) is born January 10th.
1924	Son Jurgis is born April 27th.
1926	"Gamintojas" suffers losses and stops operations. "Pienocentras" or Milk Center takes over.
1932	Mother-in-law Sofija Zuboviene dies in Ginkunai at age 72.
1933	Father-in-law Vladimir Zubov dies in Medemrode at age 71. JF's wife Aleksandra inherits Ginkunai. (Medemrode property goes to V. Zubov's second wife, her step-mother.) Primary school in Ginkunai named after Sofija and Vladimir Zubov.
1940?	Ginkunai estate lands transferred to the State Land Fund/Trust.
1940	*About 20 years of independence ends.*
1940	Moves to Kaunas, Alyte & Jurgis are still in school.
1940	*June: Russia occupies Lithuania for two years; many exiled to Siberia.*
1942?	Suffers ill health. Moves to Skaudvile.
1942	*German occupation*
1944	Move to Silgaliai. Move to Trapai for 3 years. Return to Skaudvile.
1944	*Germans leave again. Jan: all of Lithuania is under Russian occupation again.*

1944   His daughter Sofija and her husband Eric Pempe
with baby Saulius leave the country, fleeing the
arriving Russian occupation.

1959   Finishes memoir.

1961   Wife Aleksandra dies at age 70.

1965   March 1st, Jonas Fledzinskas dies at age 80 in
Skaudvile.

1991   *Lithuania is independent again.*

Jonas and Aleksandra Fledzinskas Family

JONAS
FLEDŽINSKIS
1885-1965

1915

ALEKSANDRA
ZUBOVAITĖ
1891 - 1961

VYTAUTAS
FLEDŽINSKAS
1919.06.10

1942

STASĖ
LIČKŪNAITĖ
1919.05.01

ERIKAS PEMPĖ
1911.01.20 -
1990.02.15

1943

SOFIJA
FLEDŽINSKAITĖ
1920.08.03

VYTAUTAS
KAŠUBA
1915.08.15 -
1997 .04.14

1944

ALEKSANDRA
FLEDŽINSKAITĖ
KAŠUBIENĖ
1923.01.10

JURGIS
FLEDŽINSKAS
1924.04.27 -
1988.08.12

KORNELIJA
KALINAUSKAITĖ
1925.05.11

Vytautas and Stase Fledzinskas Family

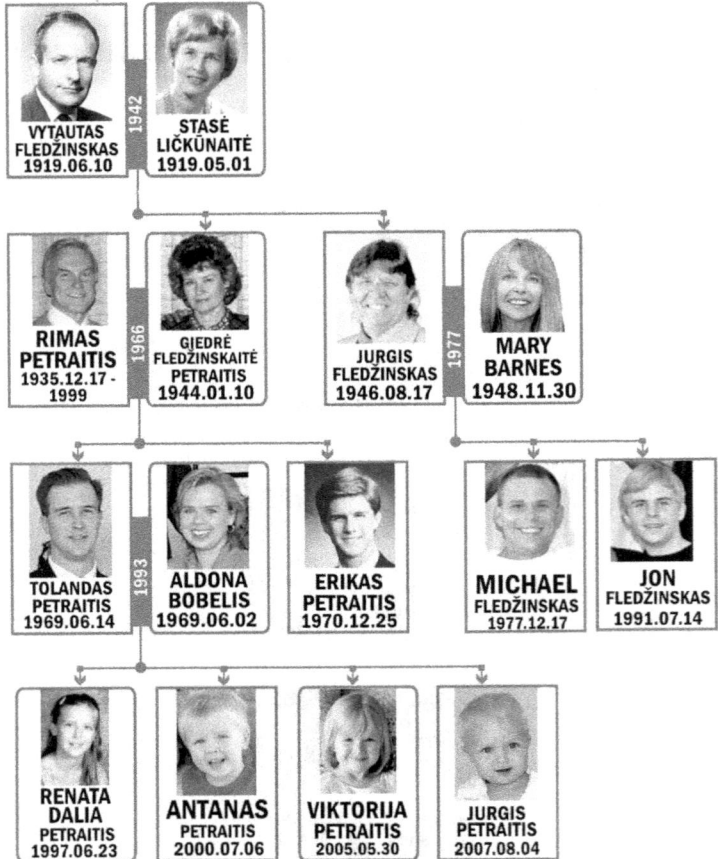

VYTAUTAS FLEDŽINSKAS 1919.06.10 — 1942 — STASĖ LIČKŪNAITĖ 1919.05.01

RIMAS PETRAITIS 1935.12.17 - 1999 — 1966 — GIEDRĖ FLEDŽINSKAITĖ PETRAITIS 1944.01.10

JURGIS FLEDŽINSKAS 1946.08.17 — 1977 — MARY BARNES 1948.11.30

TOLANDAS PETRAITIS 1969.06.14 — 1993 — ALDONA BOBELIS 1969.06.02

ERIKAS PETRAITIS 1970.12.25

MICHAEL FLEDŽINSKAS 1977.12.17

JON FLEDŽINSKAS 1991.07.14

RENATA DALIA PETRAITIS 1997.06.23

ANTANAS PETRAITIS 2000.07.06

VIKTORIJA PETRAITIS 2005.05.30

JURGIS PETRAITIS 2007.08.04

Eric and Sofija Pempe Family

ERIKAS PEMPÉ
1911.01.20 -
1990.02.15

1943

SOFIJA
FLEDŽINSKAITÉ
1920.08.03

SAULIUS
PEMPE
1943.12.27

JEFFREY
MILSTEIN

RUTA SEVO
1945.05.07

WERNER
PEMPE
1957.06.09

JOHN PEMPE
1951.05.07

1980

TERESA C.
ROBINSON
1953.01.27

PETER PEMPE
1954.03.03-
2002.11.12

1977

JOANNE
CEDERHOLM
1956.10.08

ALEX PEMPE
1988.01.30-
2007.02.07

JASON PEMPE
1979.04.18

JENNIFER
BUSSE

TOM
CHAPPELL

ELIZABETH
PEMPE
1984.10.07

Vytautas and Aleksandra Kasuba Family

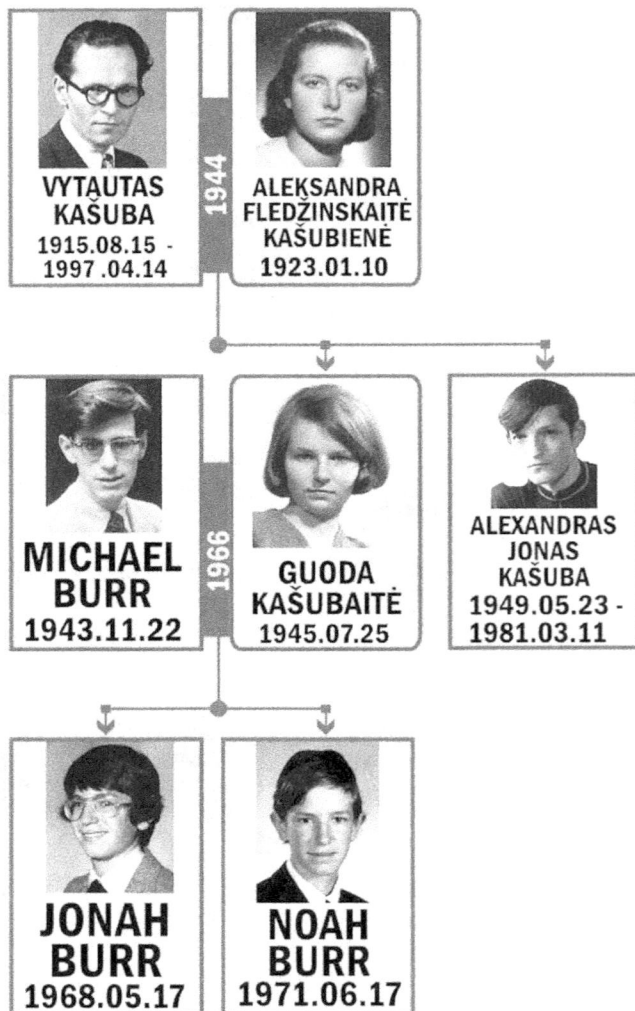

VYTAUTAS KAŠUBA
1915.08.15 -
1997.04.14

1944

ALEKSANDRA
FLEDŽINSKAITĖ
KAŠUBIENĖ
1923.01.10

MICHAEL BURR
1943.11.22

1966

GUODA
KAŠUBAITĖ
1945.07.25

ALEXANDRAS
JONAS
KAŠUBA
1949.05.23 -
1981.03.11

JONAH BURR
1968.05.17

NOAH BURR
1971.06.17

Jurgis and Cornelia Fledzinkas Family

JURGIS FLEDŽINSKAS 1924.04.27 - 1988.08.12

KORNELIJA KALINAUSKAITĖ 1925.05.11

PUTINAS FLEDŽINSKAS 1949.04.13 - 2008.11.06

1. **GIEDRĖ KRIŠČIŪNAITĖ** 1945. 10. 17

2. **REGINA SABALTAS** 1953.03.27

TAURIUS FLEDŽINSKAS 1954.05.29 - 1995.04.21

DAIVA MACKAVECKAITĖ 1952.07.25 - 2000.02.10

ALDIS FLEDŽINSKAS 1970.04.18

MILDA KUTRAITĖ 1980.04.08

2. **GUODA FLEDŽINSKAITĖ NAMAVIČIENĖ** 1980.04.08

ANDRIUS FLEDŽINSKAS 1982.10.28

JONAS FLEDŽINSKAS 1976.10.03

VIRGINIJA ŠALTYTĖ 1984.07.05

TOMAS FLEDŽINSKAS 1979.12.25 - 2007.08.24

MAGĖ FLEDŽINSKAITĖ 1992.06.20

FLEDŽINSKAITĖ UGNĖ 1999.10.22

MATIS FLEDŽINSKAS 2007.09.05

IVETA FLEDŽINSKYTĖ 2007.01.03

93

Zubov lineage (Partial)

Count Alexander Nikolajevitch Zubov 1727-1795
m. Elizaweta Wassiljiwna Voronnova 1742-1814
Titled in 1793
!

Count Dimitry Alexandrovich Zubov 1764-1836
m. Praskovja Alexandrovna Viazemskaja 1772-1835
!

Count Nikolajus Zubov 1801-1871
m.Aleksandra Raimon-Moden 1807-1839
!

Count Nikolajus Nikolaevicius Zubov 1832-1898
m. Alexandra Olsufjeva 1840-1913
!

Count Vladimir Zubov 1862-1933
m. Sofija Bileviciute 1860-1932
!

Jonas Fledzinskas 1885-1965
m. Countess Aleksandra Zubovaite 1891-1961

Ionas Fledzinskas (1885-1965) and Aleksandra Zubovaite-Fledzinskiene (1889-1960)

ca 1938

Alexandra Zubovaite-Fledzinskiene 1889-1960 ca 1938?

Jonas
Fledzinskas
1885-1965

Jonas Fledzinskas 1885-1965

Jonas Fledzinskas 1885-1965

ca 1933

Jonas Fledzinskas, son Jurgis and his son

Aleksandra Zubovaite-Fledzinskiene 1891-1961
ca 1912 in Berlin

Aleksandra Zubovaitė ir
Sofija Bilevičiūtė - Zubovienė. Apie 1909

Aleksandra
Zubovaite-Fledzinskiene
1891-1961

Fledzinskas Family ca. 1930

Aleksandra Fledzinskiene with Jurgis and Aleksandra

Aleksandra, Vytautas, Jurgis, Sofija Fledzinskas

Aleksanda, Vytautas, Sofija, and nanny?

Sofija Bileviciute-Zuboviene with four grandchildren ca. 1924

Sofija Zuboviene, Vytautas, Aleksandra, Sofija

Sofija and Aleksandra Fledzinskaite

Aleksandra, Jurgis, Sofija, Vytautas Fledzinskas

Ginkunai patio

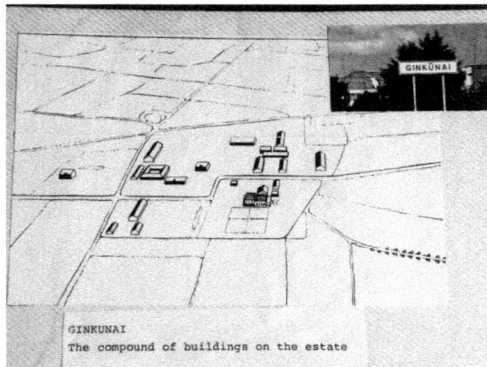

GINKUNAI
The compound of buildings on the estate

Fledzinskas family:
mother Roze Jokubauskaite-Fledzinskiene, Jonas,
Stanislava, Juzefa, Vytautas, and Ona.
Father Antanas not in picture. ca 1895

Sofija Bilevičiūtė-Zubovienė 1860-1932
This photo is displayed in schools founded by the Zubovs

Sofija Bilevičiūtė-Zubovienė's gravesite
"Here lies ... Died in Ginkūnai
1932 June 9th, 72 years old

Vladimir Zubov 1862-1933

Vladimir Zubov
My Grandfather
1862-1933

Vladimír Zubov 1862-1933

Hipolit Billevicz   1822-1901
Father of Sofija B-Zuboviene
(Father-in-law to Vl. Zubov)

Philosopher and writer

Elena Daugirdaite-Billevicz 1841-1940
Wife of Hipolit Billevicz
Mother of Sofija B-Zuboviene   ca 1887

Daughter of Nikolajaus N Z, sister of Vl Zubov

Olga Zubov 1889-1902

Son of Nikolajus N.Zubov,
Brother of Vl. Zubov

Dimitri Zubov

Daughter of Nikolajus,
Sister of Vl. Zubov

Marija Zubov
Maried Tolstoj

PHOTO-CRAYON

VIL.

1832-1898
Nikolajus Nikolaevičius Zubovas
apie 1890 metus   Father of Vl. Zubov

111

Alexandra Zubov 1840-1913
Wife of Nikolaievitch Z, born Olssufiew

Nikolaievitch Zubov
1832-1898
Father of Vl. Zubov

Alexandra Zubov 1840-1913
Wife of Nikolaiev ich, born Olssufiew

Wife of Nikolajus Nikolaievicius Zubov

Alexandra Zubov 1840-1913
Wife of Nikolajus Nikolaevicius Zubov

Dimitry Alexandrovitch
Zubov
1764-1836
Son of Alexander
Nikolaievitch

Praskovja Alexandrovna
Zubova
Born Pricess Wjasemskaja
1772 - 1835
Wife of Dimitry

Alexander Nikolajevitch
Zubov
17.. – 17..
Father of Dimitry Alexandrovitch Zubov

Elizaweta Wassiljiwna
Zubova
Born Woronowa
1742 – 1814
Wife of Alexander

Gyvenamasis namas (Fledžinskų). XIX a. vidurys. (Tauragės g.)

Skaudvile

Fledzinskas graveside: Jonas, Aleksandra, and his sister Ona

(This short history is provided for context. It relies on various encyclopedias. It is not a reliable scholarly source. Readers who want a more accurate and complete account should refer back to other sources.)

An Early History of Shifting Status

The current geographic area that constitutes Lithuania has gone through many phases of ethnic and political dominance.

At the end of the 14th Century, the majority of the population was East Slavs, who, facing aggression from Moscow, turned to the Poles for protection. At that time, Lithuania geographically included all of Belarus and Ukraine. The official language was Old Byelorussian, not Lithuanian. The Lithuanian language was spoken by peasants, who constituted about 75% of the population and who mainly spoke Lithuanian. Polish gentry (landowners) made up about 10%, and ethnic Germans and Jews made up about 15%. Townspeople were mostly Jews, Germans, and Polish/Lithuanian gentry. Polish became the language of the upper classes, who saw themselves as both Poles and Lithuanians.

The University of Vilnius was founded in 1579 and became a preeminent educational center for eastern and central Europe.

Enter the Russians

A long period of Polish domination ended in the late 18th Century, when Poland itself was partitioned, and the Russians became rulers of the region. The Russians banned the name "Lithuania," imposed the use of the Cyrillic alphabet, and limited economic development.

By 1897 there were 2.7 million people under the Russians. About 87% lived in rural areas, 13% in town. Peasants comprised 73% of the population, townsfolk 20%, and nobles 5%. Languages: 58% Lithuanian, 13% Jewish, 10% Poles, 15% Eastern Slavic.

Clearly there were distinct cultural and linguistic communities living side by side. Many townspeople were necessarily multi-lingual. Records show that there were at least 350 shtetls, or Jewish settlements, spread throughout the region, with little interaction with others except in markets and commerce.

World War I   During World War I, the Germans gained a stronghold in the area and occupied it for three years. After the War, in February 1918, Lithuanian leaders declared the country independent. Russian efforts to reclaim the territory failed; they recognized independent Lithuania in 1920. Vilnius was named the capital, but Poles seized the city in 1920. The Lithuanian capital was moved to Kaunas.

There was increasing polarization and competition between ethnic populations in the towns. There were those speaking Polish (24%), Lithuanian (8%), and Belarussian (22%). The large Jewish population (42%) spoke Yiddish or Russian.

Less than 3% of the population of Vilnius spoke Lithuanian. It was the language of peasants and farmers -- 93% of Lithuanian-speakers were peasants; only 4% of townsfolk and 2.5% nobles. In Kaunas district, up to 6.7% of the nobles were Lithuanian-speaking.

Among Polish speakers – 41% were peasants, 30% nobles, and 26% townsfolk.

Independence 1920-1939

Following World War II, an independent Lithuania started to rebuild its infrastructure. Land reforms starting in the 1920s shifted ownership from the estate holders to the state and to cooperatives.

Nobles took a low profile, due to the threats of persecution after the Russian revolution and its distain for elite classes. To some extent the dominance of Poles among gentry contributed to the notion that the gentry were a foreign-born ruling class and landlords. Many participated in nation-building but had to overcome a history of privilege and power in the countryside.

About 28% of those who were nobles by birth and lived in the region spoke Lithuanian. The percentage of nobles speaking Lithuanian in Kaunas administrative district (the capital of Independent Lithuania) was higher: 36.6%. The majority of nobles -- 59% -- spoke Polish, so the association of nobility and Polish heritage was strong.

During this period, a complete educational system was developed. The city of Kaunas gained a university and developed other urban characteristics, serving as the capital.

Until 1940, economy was primarily agricultural – dairy farms and livestock. There were few natural resources, mostly peat and amber.

The period saw the rise of ethnic nationalism.

World War II
Russian
Occupation
1939-1942

At the start of World War II, in 1939, Germany and the Soviet Union divided up Eastern Europe, and they assigned Lithuania to Russian dominion. The Russians overthrew the independent Lithuanian ruling regime and governed it as a republic starting in 1940. Between 1940 and 1941, the Soviets deported thousands of Polish-Lithuanians to Siberia.

German
Occupation
1942-1944

In 1941, the Germans invaded and pushed the Russians out. With possible cooperation from locals, they massacred the Jewish population of 240,000 (10% of the total population), as well as Polish intelligensia.

Russian
Occupation
1944 & 1945

The Soviet army returned in 1944 and 1945. The Russians deported 150,000 individuals to Siberia – anyone considered educated, elite, or a leader , including teachers, religious figures (of any denomination), and government workers.

Vilnius as a city was altered irrevocably. The Vilna ghetto holds the memory of extreme ethnic oppression and genocide. Many remaining Poles relocated to Poland in 1946. The Lithuanian language was repressed and banned from schools and public media.

Russification took hold. The Soviets collectivized agriculture and pushed industrialization, moving more people into cities, including migrants from Soviet areas. By the 1960s, native Lithuanians started to enter the system as Communist leaders.

Around 1988, Gorbachev introduced a program of reform that encouraged local control and decentralization of satellite countries called Perestroika. His action encouraged the formation of Sajudis – the Lithuanian Movement for Perestroika. Sajudis campaigned for complete independence, beyond decentralization. The Lithuanian Community Party declared independence in December of 1989. The Sajudis-led parliament declared an independent Lithuanian state in January of 1991.

Independence 1991-

To solidify its independence, Lithuania joined NATO in November of 2002 and became a member of the European Union in 2004.

In 2001, 67.2% of the population lived in cities and 33% in rural areas. Up until WWII, most of population had been farmers and peasants.

For ethnic composition, in 2001, Lithuanians were 83% of the population, Russians 6%, and Poles 7%. There were pockets of Belarussians, Ukrainians, Tatars, Karaites, and 3,000 Romani (who survived German extermination). (Karaites are a branch of Judaism, with 250 members located mostly in Vilnius and Trakai. They speak a Turkish-based language using the Hebrew alphabet.)

In terms of religion, in 2001, 79% of the population is Roman Catholic. Others: Russian Orthodox 4%; Jews 4,000; Lutheran 20,000; Evangelical Reformed 7,000; Sunni Muslim 2,700.

Language

Sanskrit and Lithuanian are closely related linguistically, with roots in the Indo-European language transported by the Aryans to India. Lithuanian and Latvian are the oldest Indo-European languages still spoken, and have a grammar as complex as classical Greek.

www.ingramcontent.com/pod-product-compliance
Lightning Source LLC
Chambersburg PA
CBHW060210070426
42447CB00035B/2886